Fishtails

Men who bite, dates that suck,
and other cautionary tales from
a mid-life fishing expedition

Enjoy my pain!
Nani

Nanci Williams

DUB
BOOKS

NANCI WILLIAMS

For my parents.

My dad taught me how to put a worm on a hook and my mom sent me to charm school. In doing so, they provided me with the skills I need to be single, and the raw material for this book.

Fishtails
Men who bite, dates that suck, and other cautionary tales
from a mid-life fishing expedition

Nanci Williams

F I R S T   E D I T I O N

ISBN: 978-1-936214-98-3

Library of Congress Control Number: 2012949007

Cover photo: Kent Clemenco
Cover design: Mike Bohrer, Charlotte Boccone

Published by Dub Books, An Imprint of Wyatt-MacKenzie
dubbooks@wyattmackenzie.com

Table of Contents

Foreword

When I type the word "fisherwoman," spell-checker suggests I change the word to "fishwife," which is an old-world term for a woman who sells fish. The more neutral term "fisher" can only describe an animal, like a bear, that catches fish to eat. So I am a fisherman, and one need simply ignore the gender bias in the word to comprehend my tale.

I fish because my first 11 years were spent in Minnesota – land of 10,000 lakes, sky blue waters, *Lake Woebegone* days, and former Vice President Hubert Humphrey. I include the latter only because the future second-in-command under President Lyndon Johnson once kissed me as a baby, back in a day when being overly attentive to children was a proven method of getting elected, and not suspicious behavior. So you could say my 15 minutes of fame, as foretold by Andy Warhol, was over before I could even walk. But I digress.

As a child of the lake country, and the tomboy in my family of 4 girls, learning to fish was predestined. We lived a stone's throw from downtown Minneapolis; in a neighborhood best known as Mary Tyler Moore's televised stomping ground, but there were several lakes within a 15-minute drive of our home. My father and I spent many a summer Sunday in a sturdy little aluminum rowboat eating peanut butter sandwiches and fishing for walleye or crappy, (which are good eating fish, *dontchaknow*.) Later in life, I married a fellow ex-Minnesotan, and we bought a house on a lake in California so he could spend weekends fishing for the elusive California golden trout, and I would resume my childhood avocation by joining him. We were good together then. Me with a book, he with his music, both of us eating our peanut butter sandwiches as we trolled – the boat gently rocking us into a false sense of forever-ness.

For those who did not grow up on a lake; are not from Minnesota; have never owned a boat; and buy their fish wrapped tightly in cellophane to lock in the odor, I offer the following glossary of fishing terms. The narrative of single life is best relayed through the lexicon of a fisherman, and I am a fisherman.

Glossary

Fishing: *v.* 1. The avocation of searching for a soul mate. 2. A metaphor for seeking a better life.

Fish: *n.* A single man. *v.* Present-tense form of fishing, i.e., *I fish, therefore I am.*

Fisherman: *n.* 1. One who engages in fishing. 2. A single woman.

NANCI WILLIAMS

The Pond: *n.* 1. Where one finds fish. 2. Usually refers to a dating website called *Plenty of Fish*.

Livewell: *n.* A vessel in which fish are kept alive while decisions are made. 2. An email in-box or a cell phone contacts list.

Lure: *n.* An object used to attract fish, e.g., a sparkly top worn in an on-line profile photo. 2. A seductive tone in the profile itself.

Bait: *n.* Any item that will elicit response from a fish, e.g., a pithy email or an alluring photo. *v.* The act of placing bait, as *to bait a hook*.

Worm: *n.* A specific item of living bait, which is proven to elicit response from a fish when it wiggles.

Hook: *n.* Device used to capture fish and remove them from the pond. Usually hidden with bait, and camouflaged by a lure. *v.* The act of securing a fish for removal from the pond, i.e. *once you hook a fish.*

Trolling: *v.* 1. Motoring across a lake or pond with a line in the water. 2. Walking through a bar or crowded room wearing an alluring outfit.

Sportfishing: *v.* 1. The avocation of searching for a soul mate, with no intention of securing a soul mate. 2. Seeking a sex partner for the evening.

Fishtail: *n.* 1. The back end of a fish; usually its most attractive feature. 2. Cocktails shared by fishermen when they are talking about men, i.e., *Meet me later for fishtails.*

NANCI WILLIAMS

Many go fishing all of their lives without knowing
that it is not fish they are after.

Henry David Thoreau

NANCI WILLIAMS

1

Fishing at Fifty

Single men are like fish. They travel in schools, only bite if the worm wiggles, frighten easily, and have the attention span of, well... a husband. My own soon-to-be-ex-husband's fleeting passions often brought to mind the voiceover of an underwater fishing documentary I once watched with my dad: *See how the fish is attracted to the shiny lure? See how the fish moves from lure to lure, until the scent of fresh bait distracts him? Look what happens when there are many lures in the water... some of the fish get over-stimulated and swim away.*

For me becoming single at middle age wasn't the heartbreak you read about in books or see in movies. It was invigorating – like a fresh start on adulthood to launch the countdown to my 50th birthday. I finally got to furnish the house the way I wanted, walls painted in bright colors and adorned with art that reflected my taste for bold and contemporary. When my husband lived here, it was room after room of compromise; his images of ducks in flight hanging side-by-side with my large abstract paintings, coexisting in a negotiated peace, like *my* cat and *his* dog.

I've always been independent, and that might explain my three failed marriages. I hear women talk in "we" about their husband and family is if they have one brain and one collective opinion. "*We're* so happy in our new home," "*We* are supporting Obama for president," "American Idol is *our* favorite show." It's like the way a school of fish will swim along together and suddenly make a hard right turn, or a complete turn-around, at the exact same moment. My brain just isn't wired that way, and when I try to speak in the royal "we" it feels unnatural and sometimes makes me laugh. I am the lone fish who strays to play with a wiggly worm... the one who gets caught. The one who gets left behind.

My older sister Dana, who lives in Las Vegas, has never been left behind. Divorced for three years, and highly adept at Internet dating, she convinced me to jump into "the pond" within days of becoming single. Over the telephone one night, she helped me to write a profile she called my *lure*, and we selected photos from my Facebook page that made me appear mid-wiggle instead of mid-life. We talked about the type of *fish* I would catch, went over the kind of *bait* I should use, and she gave me short instruction on when to set the *hook*. The fishing metaphors *fly* when you're on a dating site called *Plenty of Fish*.

"It's never too soon to get in the game," she told me, and my line was in the water with one click of the upload button. I stared at the screen while I wondered if taking advice from my cougar sister, a former Vegas showgirl, was a good idea. Her tutelage would have me donning a feather headdress and chasing a stagehand half my age around a dressing room, I feared. Dana and I had nothing in common and never had. I was short and she was tall; I was the smart one, she was the beauty; I was the tomboy, she was the girly-girl; I was the writer, she was the performer. Still, our life-long differences did not prevent my older sister from assuming authority over my mid-life transition and insisting she become my dating coach.

Shortly after I published my on-line profile (or *baited the hook*) a school of *fish* swam up to nibble – just like my sister told me they would, and just like the schools of fish did in that old underwater fishing film my dad showed me as a kid. My *livewell* filled up quickly because I was the latest arrival to this friendly fish party, so it took considerable time to sort through my haul for the day and decide who was edible and who would be thrown back. I wrote something pithy to everyone who nibbled, but only sent personal wiggly notes to a few chosen fish.

"I see you are a skier. I am too! Where do you usually go?"

"You say you're a guy who likes to tinker around your house. Maybe you could come over with your toolbox?"

"Are you wearing a San Jose Sharks jersey in your profile photo? That's fantastic because I am a HUGE hockey fan – Go Sharks!"

The remaining hopefuls got a friendly rejection note to read as I gently removed the hook: "Thanks for taking the bait, but I'm going to keep fishing."

Several hours later, some of the released fish have refused to leave my livewell, and not one of the chosen few had responded. They were gone – hooked by another line in the water. According to Dana, I took too long crafting my wiggly notes and didn't respond fast enough. "The good fish get caught quickly," she told me.

The trend continued into the next day: fish on/fish off, fish on/fish off, fish on/fish off. Who knew that fishing was fast moving, highly competitive, and full of heart-pumping excitement? I called Dana after several hours of working the pond.

"Answering all these emails takes up so much time," I said. "How do you find time to date?" Dana laughed, and explained that the quantity of fish would go down in a few days.

"You can afford to be picky in the beginning," she told me. "Think about what you're looking for in your next relationship, and don't settle for anything less."

What am I looking for in my next relationship? I wondered. *What was I looking for in my last relationship?* "Am I even looking for a relationship?" I asked her.

"Of course you're looking for a relationship," Dana said. "We all are, it's just that some of us are holding out for a perfect relationship and others are willing to settle for anyone with a pulse."

I am still new to being single, and indulging in my independence, but Dana is probably right that I will feel differently when the loneliness settles in. She's been looking for the perfect relationship for three years, and hasn't found it yet. Of course, she's looking

NANCI WILLIAMS

for someone half her age with all the wisdom and financial security that comes with a man much older. The man I would be looking for is a little more like a male version of myself, which would make him very independent, and probably not willing to settle down. For the first time in our lives, my sister Dana and I have something in common: we are fishing the same pond, and each trolling for a different but equally rare breed of fish.

On my second day on the Internet I caught my first fish. He used football references in his profile, so chatting on-line was easy. "It's halftime, and important decisions have to be made," he wrote. I kept the football metaphor going in my response by saying that I too was standing on the 50-yard-line and contemplating my next play. I made a date to meet "Football Bob" for coffee, and the conversation was easy.

"You look exactly like your picture," he said when I took the seat across from his at Starbucks.

"You do too," I said, noting to myself that we had both worn jeans with the same color shirts. Already we looked like one of those couples that dress alike to show the world they are together.

"Please tell me you voted for Obama," he inquired, indicating that political leaning was a priority to him.

"I did vote for Obama, and I can't tell you how glad I am that you asked first!"

We had much in common, and reached the end zone together with time left in the 3rd quarter. Our coffee date discussion revealed that Football Bob and I both liked Asian food of all kinds; drove the same model car; both loved to ski; shared similar values and political beliefs, and had the same birthday. Except for his obsession with football (which I hate) Bob was looking very much like my male counterpart, and I quietly marveled at the speed and ease with which I had caught this very edible fish on my second day in the pond.

Football Bob and I swam around together for a little over a week, but he managed to free himself of my hook after the fourth date, saying he needed to get back on the field. He said he would know by now if I was following his game plan, and he didn't see a position for me on the team. In short, he wasn't feeling *it*.

Game plan? Team? After a week? To use another football analogy, it felt like Bob was already a star quarterback while I was still scratching my head and thinking - *Should I play offense or defense?* If I had known I was still in try-outs, and hadn't made the roster, I would have *played* the game, instead of lingering near the sideline in hopes that someone would want my autograph.

The thrill of victory; the agony of defeat. All sports clichés apply.

I headed to the locker room to consult my coach-sister, who again gave me the *faster, faster* pep talk, followed by a butt slap and orders to return to the pond. "Fish are biting NOW!" Dana said, "and one of them could be your perfect catch."

I returned to the pond, got my line in the water, and started pulling out fish. My first bite was an "active

79-year-old who loves to golf and ski." That could have been my dad, but it probably wasn't, because my dad's still married to my mom. The next fish was 18 years old and said he was "very mature and has a car and no curfew." This could have been my nephew Travis, but the nephew who lives with me hasn't said that many words to me in months. My dry cleaner wanted to date me... my dad again... my soon-to-be-ex-husband's best friend... my dad again... my dad again... yet another Bob (even their names are fishing terms.)

"Bob2" and I exchanged phone numbers and agreed to meet for a drink later that day. He said he was 48 years old, but he didn't look a day over 30 in his profile photo. I soon learned that he wasn't just aging well. Bob2 turned out to be a 26-year-old minnow with a perverse fondness for older women, who said I resembled one of his mom's friends who starred in erotic dreams he had as a teenager. While I love the idea of being someone's fantasy woman, I was not thrilled to know that being as old as his mom was the primary requisite for landing the role to play Bob2's dream girl.

The date ended early, so I paid for the drinks (age before gender); walked him to his '98 Jeep Wrangler; and gave him a brief coaching about playing fair, good sportsmanship, and something about him being a fan in the stands while I am in the game and on the 50-yard-line. I gave Bob2 a motherly pat on the head as I gently removed the hook and sent him home.

Dana didn't get it. She screamed on the phone, "you released him?!?!"

"Yes," I told her. "It seemed the humane thing to do."

"You caught and released a 26-year-old fish?" she asked. "Was he cute? Did he have a good job?" When my answer was "yes" to both questions, my cougar sister hung up on me in disgust.

I returned to the pond and found a school of minnows in my livewell. I wondered if I should change bait. The animal print top I was wearing in my profile photo – the one Dana picked out – screamed *cougar*. I scrapped it and went in search for another. While contemplating lures I looked at the scoreboard and my heart started pounding with adrenaline as the words of my coach shouting *faster, faster* rang in my ears, and the knowledge that I had to decide quickly if any of these fish were going to play on my team sunk in. Always one to bow out under pressure, I turned off my laptop and went to bed.

That night I had a wild dream. I was on a football field surrounded by giant fish wearing jerseys, pads and helmets. I didn't recognize the team insignia, but the uniforms allowed their enormous fish tails to remain exposed, and they used them to knock each other over on the field. *Whoosh!* A player was down. *Whoosh!* Another fish lie flopping on the field. I was inappropriately dressed in cut-off jeans, a pink tank top and the little beige fishing vest I used to wear as a kid; completely unprotected from the brutality of my opponents.

Halftime was almost over... A school of fish was coming my way... I needed to decide immediately whether I was going to play offense or defense… and I couldn't seem to get the worm to stop wiggling so I could bait my hook. I looked up just in time to see a fish coming my way in tackle position. Reaching for the only defense I had at my disposal, I hit him as hard as I could with my metal tackle box. He went down.

A referee was blowing his whistle at me… YOU'RE OUT! The call? Traveling.

Traveling? We were playing *basketball* now? Dreams are like that, but I was never good at dribbling.

It seems that traveling meant *traveling* in this bizarre game of fishing-at-fifty, because I was thrown off the field for carrying too much baggage. "It's weighing you down," yelled the ref. "You have no speed, girl!"

I am bolder in my dreams than in real life, so I got in the ref's face. "Hey, we all have baggage," I screamed, "we're middle aged, for God's sake!"

I kept going. "Isn't that what fishing at fifty is all about? You bring your baggage, they bring their baggage, and you unpack together – item-by-item – to see if it's possible to get it all into one suitcase?" The ref looked at me quizzically, reminded me that we were playing *football*, and upheld his call. So I was OUT.

I awoke the next morning remembering the dream and decided it was a sign. I had no business fishing when I didn't feel like fish for dinner. I was carrying too much baggage from my recent break up to run from metaphor to cliché with speed and agility. I was simply not ready to start dating again.

That first plunge into the pond was only a few days

after my husband of 20 years walked out, so I was all of three weeks single when I hung up my rod and reel by disabling my on-line profile after my second week in the pond. I had been in one relationship after another since I was 16 years old and if Football Bob hadn't released me, that pattern may have continued. I decided then my time would be better spent painting another wall in my house orange or maybe red, and putting it on the market.

As my dad used to say when my mom would make me clean my room before I could go to the lake – "The fish will just have to wait until we get our house in order."

2
Monogamy

The color left his face the instant I struck him, but he still answered his cell phone – seemingly unaware that a crimson imprint of my right hand was beginning to form on the left side of his face. I had never slapped a man before, and made mental note of my observation that a violent act could cause no pain when the assault was anticipated. I make a lot of mental notes about the behavior of men, as part of my ongoing sociological studies. You would think I would have been a perfect wife for all the stored knowledge I have accumulated on the subject.

Sociology is not my life's work but I dabble in it from time to time. You could say it was my subject of interest in the 12 or so years I was going to college part-time, because I was strangely drawn to class titles like *Gender Roles in Interpersonal Relationships; Man: a Social Creature*; and *Sexual Deviance in our Society.* Around the advent of my 30th birthday I decided it was time to start my real life, so I queried my guidance counselor as to which of my abandoned majors would get me degreed and out of there fast. "Sociology," he said, and I now hold a college degree in the Scientific Study of Human Social Behavior; due mostly to the semi-perverted party girl I was in my twenties.

As an amateur sociologist I have collected and reviewed a great deal of clinical, statistical and anecdotal data on the behavior of men, in addition to my own work in the field. Anthropologists have long believed the male of the human species is simply not hard-wired for monogamy, and that fact is well documented in the book *Sex at Dawn: The Prehistoric Origins of Modern Sexuality* by Christopher Ryan and Cacilda Jetha published by Harper Collins in 2010. This groundbreaking book on natural primates notes that female Homo-sapiens are not monogamous by nature either; but I believe the practice of raising children – which puts women in hotel bars significantly less often than the male of the species – can be cited as the primary cause for statistical oneness falling on the male in modern times.

Men are genetically programmed to spread their seed far and wide, and are intrinsically cognizant of the offspring potential in the mates they choose. Sperm fish instinctively sense that younger partners are better for bearing and carrying children, and somehow know the eggs of fairer-featured females are less inclined to absorb the negative genetic traits naturally propagated by males. It's a scientific fact: by their very nature, men cheat.

I am not one of those hysterical females – less educated in the science of human behavior – holding the belief that cheating husbands are "dogs" and should be castrated when caught. I am a sociology scholar who sees monogamy as a lofty goal, and not a natural way of living one's life. Our puritanical society tends to ostracize natural humans, labeling them adulterers and forcing them to hide in cheap motel rooms or on Utah farms. Yet we do absolutely nothing to celebrate the few among us who are successfully practicing monogamy.

I have many male friends whom I believe are monogamists. Whether they are monogamous for lack of opportunity; whether they are upholding the values of their faith; or whether they are just really, really afraid of their spouses is not important. What is noteworthy is they have reprogrammed their brain to do something every cell in their body says is unnatural; for which they should be sainted, or celebrated with a parade, or held up in some meaningful way for civilized society to see they are better human beings than most. For a case in point, look to the singular challenge of climbing Mount Everest. Those who are successful in climbing 29,000 feet are applauded for overcoming their body's natural tendency to die at high altitudes and to be very, very afraid of heights. Should we chastise every human being who has not and cannot climb Mount Everest? I think not.

It was not the sociologist and highly-evolved female I know myself to be who slapped my husband so hard it left my handprint on the side of his face when his girlfriend called in the middle of delivering his "you're great, but I'm leaving" speech. I already knew about Marina, so this was not anger at learning she existed. The slap, and the rage that caused it, was something I had never experienced before: it was pure, unadulterated jealousy.

I was not jealous of Marina for being more desirable to my husband than me, as one might expect. I was jealous of him for being so happy that he actually glowed when he saw her name on his phone; for finding the love of his life at 56 years of age; and for feeling something so profoundly life-affirming he was willing to abandon almost everything to make it last. So complacent he was in disposing of marital assets accumulated over 20 years, all of which seemed of no consequence. "You can have all the animals... Travis can stay with you... I don't care about the stuff... you keep the house... I see no reason we can't continue working together..." the more conciliatory he was, the more jealous I became.

He was still my very competent business partner in the advertising agency we formed together shortly after we met, and co-parent to the 17-year-old nephew we had raised since he was 4. Therefore, my very livelihood and parental authority were at stake, so I would have to get over my incapacitating negative emotions to move on, and I did. It took only a day or so – and a lot of vodka – for the rage to subside, and our professional and personal relationship returned to a surprisingly productive routine, considering the circumstances.

Truth is, I didn't know I was unhappily married until I wasn't anymore. Unhappy, that is. At some point my marriage became comfortable, predictable and non-essential. I created a life outside of my marriage that I found fulfilling, and my husband did the same. Musicians, promoters and fans became his tight circle of friends after he formed a band. I got involved in politics, the local chamber of commerce, and found a growing number of girlfriends who enjoyed traveling, playing golf and going to spas. When I didn't have other plans, I got into the habit of ending the day with a cocktail long before my marriage ended, and I used it as an extension of the workday. People I used to meet for lunch got moved to end of day, because it was easier to get through any day that concluded with a pink drink and someone to talk to. This new routine also enabled me to work out at the Club at lunch, because my mid-life crisis – which kicked in at the age of 48 – manifested as an obsessive need to stay fit. With the exception of "family night," the one day a week we pledged to both come home and have dinner with Travis, you would seldom find either of us at home on any given night of the week. (The weekly dinner rule fell by the wayside too, eventually becoming "Travis night," which meant that one of us had to come home to have dinner with Travis, and we alternated the responsibility.)

I no longer defined my existence by the quality of my marital state, and I assumed my husband was of the same mindset. I had robust friendships, a satisfying career and an active social life. A good life, married to a decent man I had little in common with. Every so often the subject of marriage counseling would come up, but neither of us would follow through and make an appointment. Shortly after he left I learned he had been going to a marriage counselor alone for several weeks. I assume he was using the counselor as a sounding board for rehearsing his "you're great, but I'm leaving" speech, but I will never know for sure.

People commented all the time about how well we worked together, before and after the marriage ended. I would tell them that we both had learned to compartmentalize our professional and personal relationship, but the truth was colder than that. The passion was gone, and there was no personal relationship. My husband really was just my business partner, and a roommate who was never home, so keeping marital spats out of the office wasn't an issue.

It wasn't always that way, and I have spent many sleepless nights lately trying to put my finger on the exact moment in time when our marriage really ended. I honestly think we had a very good 10 years, but it may have been 12 or 13. It's difficult to identify the exact point in time when my life partner moved from the center of my universe to the orbit of my existence. He says it was me who checked out first, and I say it was him, but neither of us can substantiate our claim because our marriage didn't end with arguments and incidents; just a slow fade like the ending of a Barry Manilow ballad.

The agency always came first for us, and that may have been our downfall. We decided early on that I would run the company, and he would be responsible for bringing in clients. Often my role as CEO ran counter to my role as supportive wife. When he would lose a client, or we didn't prevail on an important pitch, it would be my job as CEO to ask why, and explore ways to improve the presentation. The role of a salesman's wife is to prop him up when he comes home from work after a big loss – no questions asked. *Let me take your shoes; let me give you a nice meal; let me tell you how wonderful you are and remind you that I chose you even if they didn't, and that I will stand by you through richer and poorer.* The wives who talk like that don't have to make payroll on the middle and last day of every month, or otherwise risk going to jail. In retrospect, I don't believe it is possible for two roles to run more counter; except for perhaps being your child's teacher, or working at the hospice in which your spiritual mentor is dying.

So the transition from life partners to business partners was an easy one, and we were getting along fairly well when Marina dumped him after only a month. I couldn't help but feel really bad for him. I wasn't about to reconcile, and our house was on the market, but I helped the situation as best I could by picking out the clothes I thought he should wear on dates and then making a few suggestions on women to call. (Maybe the part of his speech where he said I was "controlling" was a little true.)

I would have done anything to get the happy, confident business partner back to replace this sniveling, heart-broken shell of a man that Marina had left in my care. I so wanted to call her and inform her of our family's newly conceived "you break him, you own him" policy, but she had fled the state of California and changed her cell phone number. It seems the citizenry of my large circle of friends weren't very kind to

Marina for breaking up my marriage. Home wrecking is still frowned upon in our society – even though, in our case, the home should have been red-tagged for demolition – and Marina found it impossible to live in this town wearing that label.

So my soon-to-be-ex and the woman of his dreams did not live happily ever after. But Marina did us both a great service, really. My husband and I got out of a marriage that we were too bound by responsibility to leave on our own accord; and two people who have been in serial relationships our entire adult lives are now single for the first time (and deservedly so, for the lack of effort either of us made in the unions.)

Ironic to think how my long-held academic assumption that men were programmed to cheat, coupled with his salesman's optimism for fairy tale endings, did not prevent our marriage from becoming the casualty of an adulterous relationship. Knowing something is likely to happen does not prevent it from happening, unless you do something with the information at hand. Even when it became evident my husband was seeing another woman I did nothing, except buy some of that eyelash-growing tonic as if stubby lashes had caused my husband to stray. All I did in earnest, really, was brace myself; much like a skydiver prepares for a jump by meticulously packing his parachute and checking all the lines.

I was completely ready on August 3, 2009 – just 38 days after my husband met Marina and 21 days after I learned of their affair – when my partner in work and life walked into my office after everyone had left and said "we need to talk." The push out of the airplane was gentle and the free-fall exhilarating; a combination of fear and adrenaline mixed with euphoria, excitement and – most of all – an overwhelming sense of relief. It was over, and it was not by my hand. I could finally stop pretending my husband and business partner was still my soul mate when our shared passions had faded many years earlier. So I sat, batting my new eyelashes, and listened to him deliver a speech he had obviously rehearsed about the many wonderful things we had shared in 20 years, ending with his assertion that it was time to "move on."

It was like hitting the ground with straight legs when his cell phone rang and the rage came over me, and the ensuing slap did not seem to alarm him at all. It was only me who was surprised to learn that somewhere deep inside of my hyper-responsible CEO façade enough passion remained to be angry and jealous, if even for just a moment.

3
Man Jose

Except for a three-year stint in New York in the eighties, I have lived most of my adult life in San Jose, California, which is the "Capital of Silicon Valley" and the 10th largest city in the United States. This surprises outsiders since San Francisco, a close but smaller in size neighbor to the north with a more recognized brand overshadows San Jose. My hometown is also confused for the city of the same name in Latin America, which also enjoys better brand recognition than the one in California. Even though the technology that makes Internet commerce possible was pretty much invented here, it is impossible to make airline reservations through *Travelocity* or *Priceline* without specifying that you want to fly into San Jose, *California,* and not the capital of Costa Rica.

But everyone in the world knows Silicon Valley. They don't know where it is exactly but they have, at least, heard of the place.

San Jose city officials, and those tasked with filling hotel rooms and populating attractions, struggle with the Silicon Valley moniker. Incongruent to have an internationally-recognized nickname; to be the economic engine for the region; to boast a pretty decent hockey team; and to have just about the most pleasant weather imaginable, and to not be able to come up with a better slogan than "Tenth Largest City." Yup – that's our tagline. It replaced "Capital of Silicon Valley" a couple years ago.

Ask a local to describe San Jose and they will tell you there are lots of jobs, and that we are close to San Francisco, Monterey Bay, Yosemite, and Lake Tahoe. The distraction of having so many fabulous places to go on the weekends is perhaps the reason there is nothing to do in San Jose except work, because there's always a dozen or so hot technology start-ups looking to staff up. More patents are issued to San Jose inventors than any other city in the free world, after all.

It's a shame that technology is all the region is known for, because you just can't help but love the weather. Coming from Minnesota, and then New York, I can attest to the fact that the weather in San Jose is remarkably, astoundingly and magically temperate. Not too hot, not too cold, zero humidity, no bugs... just about as pleasant as air can get. Drive just 40 miles to San Francisco, and the weather will drop as much as 30 degrees, due to coastal fogs that stop short at the valley floor.

A modicum of native San Joseans (the city grew from a population of 30,000 to just under a million in a short 50 years) have no concept of weather being a factor in making plans. Outdoor weddings are planned for April, since the odds of rain showers are slim - and a pop-up canopy will keep the drizzle out just in case. Still these oh-so-rare natives can be found complaining about the weather on occasion when the temperature fails to get over 72 degrees in April. The rest of us just walk around smiling, and conversations often start with a story about how dreadful the humidity was in Fort Lauderdale or Houston or Kansas City or... whatever extreme weather habitat we once had to endure.

San Joseans generally make more money than their counterparts elsewhere, but a big chunk of it is spent on housing. A turn of the century bungalow downtown can carry a million dollar mortgage, and most everyone I know keeps a second home so they can live somewhere else on the weekend. But high housing prices are necessary for keeping the rest of the world from relocating to San Jose, which would result in a geological disaster of a magnitude the world has never seen, so we don't complain.

Perhaps the most startling San Jose fact is this: it is one of only a handful of cities wherein the population of men to women is significantly tilted toward the former. In the entire United States, there are 97 men for every 100 women. In San Jose, the ratio is 117 men to 100 women. The weekly newspaper once dubbed it "Man Jose," which I think has slogan potential that would serve the City better than this "We're number 10!" tagline we latched on to.

Evidence of man-heaviness is not immediately apparent to the uninitiated. On my very first night out as a single person, I had exactly the opposite experience in fact. My single friend Vicki thought I needed to "get out there," so she suggested we go to some bars in the nearby trendy suburb of Los Gatos. We did, and our first stop was a popular restaurant/bar called *Steamers*, which I was familiar with because it had existed longer than my last marriage. We walked in and the bar was jam-packed with people. We felt lucky to have nabbed the last table, but once seated noticed the entire bar area – without exception – was filled with women. There was not a hint of testosterone in the air, and no evidence we were crashing some kind of a women's convention. Each table had two or three women at it, all dressed like us, and all looking like they were single and trying to "get out there." We left before ordering a drink, because we're both independents and not inclined to join a flock of sheep. All these women were just like us: predictably doing what society expects us to do because we're single – put on our lucky blouse, grab a girlfriend or two, and GET OUT THERE!

Steamers is in the suburbs, which is where most women are left stranded when their husbands move on. Downtown restaurants are mostly filled with conventioneers and business travelers, so it is not uncommon to see a preponderance of men on any given night of the week, but they're not local and they have work to do. I like to saunter through the dining room of *The Grill on the Alley* on any weeknight, just to walk by table after table of men having dinner together. Table of 8 men... table of 6 men... table of 3 men... a couple... table of 6 men again. It's as puzzling to me as the solution to a math equation that a city with the statistical disparity of San Jose would not be an excellent place to live if you're single and female, but it's not.

To understand "Man Jose" culture, one has to get into the heart of where the men are, which is where they work. Tech companies tend to cluster together, and only a few of them are located downtown. Technology workers are sequestered on campuses of tilt-up buildings with their own recreational facilities, their own cafeteria with better food than most restaurants, their own little village squares, and – lastly – their own personal work environments equipped with everything one needs to work a 48-hour shift. Isolation from the outside world – a world that includes women – is apparently mandatory for technological genius to occur.

This sequestered nerd mentality that Silicon Valley men are world-renown for is best described in a story that won two local men fame in 2007. These two research scientists left their campus work environment to attend a seminar on "How to Flirt With Women" one summer evening in 2006. That seminar was held downtown and participants were urged to put their new skills to work immediately by going to a bar right away. In route to "getting out there," the men saw four orange glowing objects – the San Jose Semaphore atop the Adobe, Inc. headquarters building – and were mesmerized. (The four divided spheres look a little like the slightly parted lips of women in orange lipstick puckered for a kiss, so you can see how two men in search of female companionship could be confused.)

The semaphore installation was commissioned by software giant Adobe, and installed as part of the

ZeroONE digital art festival held here the year before. Designed by digital artist Ben Rubin, it emits a visual and audio code so complex, it was not fathomable that it could easily be deciphered. The condo I moved to after the house sold offers a perfectly aligned, unobstructed view of the semaphores, and I have sat for hours trying to see a pattern develop, without success. (Math-doing gives me a headache, so it's just as well.)

The two students of "flirtology" soon decided to derail their women-seeking activities to concentrate on decoding the semaphores. It took only a year of dedicated work for them to discover that the glowing orange lights were emitting the entire text of a Thomas Pynchon novel written in 1960 titled *The Crying of Lot 49*. The futuristic science fiction adventure is set in a fictitious California City filled with high-tech industrial parks and the kind of engineering sub-culture we now associate with Silicon Valley. *The Crying of Lot 49* follows a central character's discovery of latent symbols and codes embedded in the landscape and in local culture, supposedly by members of a polyamory cult.

The research scientists became the stuff legends are made of, making the front page of the *San Jose Mercury News* and receiving a lifetime supply of free software from Adobe. Ben Rubin is supposedly working on a new code, but it will take years for him to come up with something undecipherable to the citizens of Man Jose. An excerpt from the journal kept during the deciphering year is pasted below, and the complete text can be found on-line, which is where most men from San Jose spend the bulk of their free time.

```
[-\|- \|\- -/|- \-\- |/-- |/-- ||\- -/--][\-\-]
[--/- /-/- \|\- \\\- -/|- /-/- \\\-][-\|- \|\-
/-/- /\-- \|\- ///- -/|-][--|- ///- ///- /|/-]
[-\/- \-|- \|\- /\-- /\-- \\\- -/|-][\|\- -/|-]
[/-/- ///- |\-- \\\- /-\-]
```

To translate for those with non-functioning left-brains like me, it means "Finally, a Sci Fi book written in my native tongue!"

So the 17 extra men in our statistical advantage, and dozens more, are too busy innovating and inventing things to waste their superpowers on dating. I saw them on *Plenty of Fish* sometimes with coded usernames I couldn't decipher, but they preferred cyber-chats to coffee dates so it was difficult to get one to take more than a nibble, no matter how much the worm was wiggling.

One night my friend Maddie and I met for cocktails at an Indian restaurant I found on *Yelp*, which was situated halfway between her home in Palo Alto and mine in San Jose. Neither of us had ever been to this restaurant/bar, but the proximity was fortuitous. Situated right in between the headquarters of Juniper Networks, Google and a major Lockheed Martin campus, it shouldn't have surprised us that this restaurant called *Faz* was the place to go for happy hour if you are a technologist, which statistically speaking means you're a male.

We were the only women in the bar, and the bar was pretty crowded. Maddie is married to a woman. She and her partner Karen have one of the few legal same-sex California marriages which took place in the narrow window of June 16 to November 4, 2008, wherein the Supreme Court had ruled in favor of marriage equality, and the right wing religious zealots had not yet organized Proposition 8, which allowed California voters to make it illegal once again.

"What a great day to be hetero," Maddie said as she perused the room, optimistic that I would surely make a love connection that night. We stayed at Faz for about two hours, enjoying two cocktails apiece, then split a couple of vegan appetizers. In that time, not one man approached, nor did anyone try to send a complimentary beverage to the only two women in the joint. Maddie surmised that her prominent wedding ring had scared away my suitors, but I knew better. These were Silicon Valley men, and they were working.

When I compare that to a similar experience from years before, I think my point will be made. My friend Suzanne and I traveled to Palm Springs to pose as a lesbian couple and check out a gay bar whose owner was considering leasing space for a similar establishment in a building that Suzanne and her husband Jim owned downtown. Jim and Suzanne like to get an idea of the kind of operation a prospective tenant operates, which makes sense when you think about it.

Palm Springs is best known for two things: world-class golf and the late Sonny Bono. It is perhaps because Sonny was once married to Cher that Palm Springs has become the unofficial Gay Capital of California over the years in terms of its ratio of gay to straight residents. It's certainly not because of the golf. While a lot of professional women golfers are known to be gay, you would never catch a self-respecting gay man in lime green plaid pants with a polka-dot hat. San Francisco is more famous for its large gay population, but there are too many heteros in residence for it to be anything like Palm Springs. (A gay man I know who keeps a second home in the desert has told me that the mid-century modern architecture is the attraction for his "people.")

After Suzanne and I checked out the gay bar, and gave it a thumbs-up for San Jose, we traveled 20 miles east to spend a night in the posh (and straight) La Quinta Resort and Spa. Little did we know we had arrived in the middle of a major Canadian golf tournament, and we were lucky to get one of the last rooms at the resort.

We made dinner reservations at our favorite La Quinta eatery, and happened upon the same restaurant where the Canadian golfers – all men – were dining. The walk from the hostess station to our table at the back of the dining room was the closest I have ever come to feeling like I was strutting down a runway wearing a lacy bra, thong and wings in a Victoria's Secret fashion show. All eyes were on the two married women dining sans husbands in a restaurant full of heterosexual men.

Before we even had a chance to look at our menus, the waiter came over to tell us that the gentlemen sitting at table 12 wanted to buy us a cocktail. We ordered drinks, waved at table 12, and went back to the menu. When the waiter brought our cocktails, there were two each, and he explained that the gentlemen at table 4 had also sent over a complimentary beverage. This pattern continued. We got a bottle of wine from table 10, table 6 paid for our entrees, and table 5 tried to buy us desert, but we hadn't saved room.

As we were leaving the restaurant (in a taxi, because all those drinks sent our way left us unsuitable to drive,) a Canuck ran out after us and said he would pay for our taxi if we would tell him where we were going. What a night.

Despite the 17-man statistical advantage, a night like the one in La Quinta would never have taken place in San Jose. You will occasionally find yourself in a room full of men – like at *Faz* or *The Grill on the Alley* – but they will be in groups talking only to each other in computer code about tackling the latest computer virus, or about how they are going to reinvent the internet again, or maybe they're working on a new code for the semaphores. Whatever they're doing, it's more important than what I am doing, which is probably just drinking vodka with my girlfriends and talking about men.

I don't know what the ratio of men to women is in Canada, and it doesn't seem to matter anyway. For the way Suzanne and I were treated on that special night in La Quinta – by men who were definitely not going to get laid that night – one has to believe that fishing is better north of the border.

4
Naked Logic

Women make bad decisions for all sorts of reasons that everyone can relate to: "I was drunk..." "He was cute..." "I needed the money..." "It was on sale." Seldom do they admit to something much more common: "I was naked." Think about it. We make the dumbest decisions of all when we find ourselves in the naked state, and this is particularly true if we're naked in public.

Thirty or so of my closest friends, who spent my 50th birthday at a boutique hotel in San Francisco, embraced the term "naked logic" on the morning after my party when we all heard about what happened to Molly. My married friend Suzanne had organized the night's activities, brilliantly creating a guest list consisting only of friends who were older than me, and it ended with breakfast on Sunday.

My friend Molly makes big bucks as the executive assistant to one of Silicon Valley's celebrity CEOs, but you would never know from the way she conducts her personal affairs that a very important man relies on her to keep his very important life organized. She became the star of my 50th birthday after party when she told us what had transpired in the six or so hours between all of us dancing at *Harry Denton's Starlight Ballroom* until closing time, and gathering again for breakfast at our hotel. Molly and her boyfriend-at-the-time had stayed in a suite with a peculiar layout; the door to the bathroom and the door to the hallway looked exactly the same and were next to each other. She got up in the middle of the night to use the bathroom, still slightly intoxicated, and found herself naked in the hallway when the door slammed shut behind her.

The clothed mind would have just pounded on the door until her boyfriend woke up to let her back in. But Molly's mind under the influence of nudity could not process information clearly. Thinking only of taking cover quickly, she ran down the hall and crouched behind a potted plant. Once safely protected by foliage, she came to the realization that she had no phone, no vodka, and no idea what room number she was in. Her naked mind was completely incapable of formulating a new plan.

She heard the elevator stop on her floor and – thinking quickly, but using naked logic – bolted for the fire escape. Once on the fire escape, she thought it would be smarter to climb down a floor or two. Or three. Now she was unable to recall what room she was in, or what floor she was on. Still naked, and now lost, she started to wonder if the best solution would be to exit on the street and feign insanity. At least the police would throw a blanket over her before they took her away – she surmised using naked logic – and surely they would give her a hospital gown at the mental institution.

It gets worse, but I will leave Molly shivering on the fire escape for now and allow you to ponder for a moment the numerous bad decisions an otherwise smart woman can make while under the influence of nudity.

My new, single residence is a lower-floor, front-facing condominium in a downtown high-rise with floor-to-ceiling glass. I dubbed it my "fishbowl," and that was before I knew that fish would soon rule my world.

Living in public as I do has forced me to become constantly aware of where I am standing when I am naked. It takes a keen mind and constant focus to maintain vigil in a fishbowl. One night, I dropped an entire can of black paint and it splashed everywhere. I immediately started cleaning paint off the hardwood floors, and then realized my clothes were covered with black paint too.

Since I thought that taking my clothes off was urgent, I did so behind the counter in my kitchen where no one could see, and so I could quickly get my clothes soaking in the big sink. Once naked and crouched behind my kitchen counter, there was no way to get to dry, clean clothes without walking the gauntlet from the kitchen to my bedroom, which would offer thousands of people walking the street outside my home an illuminated view of my naked backside. I became paralyzed, and my I.Q. dropped at a rate of about 10 points per second. (I believe this is a documented fact, and supported in biological theory. Ask any man if he has ever known a woman, no matter how educated or intelligent, to say anything wise or quotable when she is naked. And one only has to shower with a group of professional women after a workout to know that even highly-evolved females seem to only be able to converse about shampoo brands and cellulite while in the naked state.)

After the black paint spill, I did what any woman would have done under the same circumstances: I ran across my living room naked (but partially covered in black paint) and spent the next hour hiding behind a potted plant in my living room, while the paint dried on my hardwood floors.

But that's not my most embarrassing naked moment. Right after graduating high school, and before starting college, I moved back to my birthplace of Minneapolis and spent the summer working for the phone company as a directory assistance operator. I rented an apartment in a complex that had no air conditioning, and was asked to work a graveyard shift for one week in August. It turned out to be a sweltering week with the temperature over 100 degrees for several days in a row. The first three days I didn't even try to sleep during the day, because I was conducting some kind of a sleep deprivation study on myself. By day four, I was in dire need of a long nap. As tired as I was, I still couldn't sleep in the heat of my bed at high noon. So I took off all my clothes and stretched out on my back in starfish position in the only relatively cool spot in my apartment – in the entryway in front of the door on the cool tiles – and let naked logic lull my thoughtless mind to sleep.

Several hours later I awoke to a chill of cold air. I soon realized that a section of my living room had been significantly reconstructed. It was only then I remembered the note on my door the day before informing me there would be a work crew in my apartment that day to install air conditioning, and it was obvious the crew had stepped over my naked corpse to get the job done.

Later at the pool, I asked a neighbor who had been home all day how many of them there were, and how long it had taken them. "Three men, plus the building super, for an hour or so," she said. I moved out the next day, and forfeited my cleaning deposit.

My friend Linda offers the most harrowing example of how naked logic almost resulted in her untimely demise. She used to brag about her perfectly situated top-floor condo in a mid-rise building, which was ideally situated on the edge of downtown San Jose. There were no taller buildings in the vicinity, it was out of the nearby airport flight path, and the wall between her and the patio next door was high. So she could sit on her patio naked and no one could see her.

One fine morning just a few weeks before my 50th birthday party, Linda went out for some naked coffee time, and the sliding glass door locked behind her. The safest way back in was over the adjoining patio wall to pound on her neighbor's door, but the neighbor was a high-profile local politician, and Linda did not want to wake him. She instead opted to shimmy down a drain-pipe to the street below, where there were lots of bushy plants she could hide behind. But Linda never made it to the street, because the drain pipe gave way around the third floor, leaving her naked self dangling on the side of the building during the morning rush hour on a busy downtown street. A city bus driver finally came to her rescue, and borrowed a ladder from the politician neighbor to get her down safely. They blurred her girl parts when it aired on the evening news, but they did nothing to hide her face, despite her begging.

Somehow everyone at my 50th birthday weekend celebration had missed the television news that day, because we all heard Linda's harrowing story for the first time at breakfast, when she was trying to make Molly feel better.

Getting back to poor, naked Molly, she was luckily saved from public humiliation when a hotel bellman found her asleep on the fire escape and brought her a robe. He looked up her room number on the hotel computer, and said he would let her in if she showed him some identification once inside. As soon as the door to her room was open, Molly realized the ridiculousness of her ordeal and started to giggle. She gave the bellman a generous tip, and a hug, and then crawled back into bed. Her boyfriend awoke when he heard the door open, and saw Molly enter with a handsome young black man, and he saw that she was naked under her robe, and he heard her giggling, and he saw her give the young man a fairly large wad of cash, and he was concerned.

Molly had a lot of explaining to do, which was diffi-cult because naked logic is not a concept easily grasped by men. For whatever reason, men don't mind being naked. They seem to lose no brain cells when discov-ered in their naked state, and they can accomplish almost any task with or without clothes. Perhaps this is because they can cover their boy part(s) with just one hand, leaving the other free to perform a number of every day functions, such as swinging a hammer or hailing a cab, and can do so without the aid of land-scaping. Women need more than two hands to cover all the girl parts, and our inherent inability to do math under pressure most often manifests as a ridiculously lowered IQ.

In some ways, the Naked Logic supposition can apply to turning 50 too. It's harder on women than men – who simply buy a sports car or a motorcycle and go on as if nothing has changed – and we let it paralyze us more than it should. It's just a number, after all, and shouldn't mean more than 49 and-a-half, but it does. Just like being naked in public, we become more aware of people looking at us (or not looking at us, which is worse) because we make ourselves believe they only notice the crow's feet and the laugh lines, and don't see that we are just as confused as children about what we want to be when we grow up. The scared little girl is always present, except she stopped running around the house naked about the same time she grew breasts, so I will cope with turning 50 by nurturing the confused child and ignoring the number.

Fifty is the halfway point; the middle of a football

field; a word that rhymes with "nifty;" an anniversary gilded in gold; an equal opportunity at success or failure. It's all those things, but mostly it's just a big, fat, naked number.

My advice to women who find themselves turning 50, naked, and maybe living in a fishbowl is to take a deep breath and tell yourself in simple, easy to understand words, not to panic. Imagine you are wearing beautiful clothes, and picture every one else in the vicinity naked. This will help to slow the drain on brain cells and retain logic, but not enough to make major decisions. Do not attempt anything more complicated than finding your way back to your clothes if you're naked in public. Resist, if you can, the body's natural inclination to duck behind a potted plant, and walk with your head high in the beautiful clothes you are wearing because you've reached an age where you have excellent taste and the money to dress yourself well.

5

The Trouble With Princes

The DSL speed of on-line dating was more than I could handle in the first months of being single, but I didn't let that discourage me from having a social life that included men. I was determined to approach the next phase of my romantic life carefully, and to proceed with blithe indifference, so as not to rebound into a serious relationship too quickly. I had only my teen and early adult dating experiences to draw from, and didn't yet realize the prospects were slim for a strong-willed, independent-minded 50-year-old. With the exception of Football Bob, I had married every man I had ever dated. So I created rules:

1. Don't date anyone who lives or works down-town;

2. Don't date anyone who works out at my health club;

3. Don't date any of my soon-to-be-ex-husband's friends;

4. Don't date clients or vendors; and,

5. Don't go back on the Internet to meet men.

The last rule was meant to keep my new status a secret from the people in the top four rule categories. (If they don't know I am single and available, I will not have to spurn their advances, I reasoned.)

In retrospect, I was somewhat naïve at that point as to my value on the free market, and extremely unaware of how quickly news spreads when someone changes relationship status on Facebook. Now, almost two years later, I have come to realize that all the friends who assured me I would get "snapped up in no time" were just being nice.

So in the early months following my catapult into single life, I was willing to only date men from elsewhere.

My first date with a man who fits that description may have set the tone for things to come. I met him in a hotel bar in Boston, which is nearly 3,000 miles away from my home in California, and a logical place to meet an elsewhere man.

My marriage had ended in August, so my single friend Linda suggested we take a fall trip together. Linda is a self-employed website developer who has been divorced for 15 years and loves to travel. She is known to spontaneously book a trip to Bali or Brazil, usually to get over a just-ended relationship. She reasoned that visiting the northeast to experience the colors of autumn would be therapeutic for me during this time of change.

We made Boston our beachhead and took day trips to Cape Cod, Walden Pond and to the White Mountains of New Hampshire. The landscape was breathtaking – like nothing we ever see in northern California. Leaves don't change color when they are green all year, so this was foreign to Linda who is a California native. For me, the scenery was reminiscent of my childhood in Minnesota and made me feel young again. After several days of viewing awe-inspiring spectacles of color, Linda and I were open for a new adventure.

Minds open, we traveled to Salem, Massachusetts to attend a Witchcraft Festival on the last day of our northeast sojourn. We bought hats, wands and potions; and then took classes to learn how to cast spells. The afternoon was spent at a psychic fair, where for two hours we could consult with as many clairvoyant witches as our fifty dollar investment would afford.

The Wiccan psychic fair was held in a small community center that stood in sharp contrast to the majestic trees, historic clapboard architecture and adorned festival atmosphere we had experienced throughout Salem's downtown. As soon as we walked in to the 1970s-era brick building with its T-bar acoustic tile ceilings and industrial grade linoleum floors, all the magic of Salem was gone. Each witch sat at a card table with two folding chairs, and each card table was covered with cloth. Purple silk, black satin, yellow chiffon, and some less exotic fabrics – like the same red cotton tablecloth I bought at Target for $9.99. I thought that a shared taste for cheap table linens made this witch and I soul sisters, so I selected the red haired Target-shopper to be my first Wiccan advisor.

After I shuffled the Tarot cards the designated eight

times, she turned the first card over and her bulging brown eyes got bigger.

"I see a man who lives far away," she said.

"Do you mean far away from Salem or far away from San Jose?"

She shrugged and tossed her hair. I sensed her irritation at my question.

After a pause she said, "He could be either far away physically or far away emotionally."

I laughed. "Emotionally distant? Like all men!" This wasn't much help. I was hoping for a little more specificity, at least some real data that would help me find this perfect guy on Facebook or LinkedIn.

After a few more vague predictions, I moved on to my second witch's table, this one sporting a bright yellow tablecloth. Her tarot cards also indicated a man who lived far away, but I managed to get her to commit to the notion that she was speaking in a geographic sense.

"How about some map coordinates or an email address?" I asked.

Witch Number 2 gave me a blank look, and it was hard to tell if she was trying to come up with something more concrete, or just bored with the reading.

Linda saw me sitting across from a catatonic advisor and grabbed my arm.

"You need to talk to my psychic soul sister," she said, and walked me toward a woman who looked a lot like Linda, but with wild curly hair. Wiccan Linda told me a lot of things that I already knew about myself... that I was smart, independent, and stronger with words than numbers. She also said she sensed that I was experiencing some angst about my age, but I'm guessing that a psychic could say that to any woman who appeared to be over 40-years-old and they would nod their head in agreement.

The sooth-saying witches ran the gamut from a wide-eyed 20-something who smacked bubble gum while she read tarot cards, to an elderly gentleman with long, grey hair and wire-rimmed glasses who saw messages in tea. They were consistent and very specific in their fate projections for Linda. Each told her the man of her dreams was waiting for her back home in San Jose, and one witch even described what his favorite drink would be and what he would be wearing when they met on a beach. Linda's instructions were clear and easy to follow. The only consistent theme in my readings was that I would not find true love until I relocated out of California. *Don't they know I own a business?* I wondered. How would Travis, who is still in high school, factor in to my globetrotting search for a happy ending? Relocation doesn't seem like a viable option for me. I was on the right path by seeking to date elsewhere men, apparently. This much was clear.

Let me take a moment here to point out that two business owners traveled from San Jose, California to Salem, Massachusetts to attend a Witchcraft Festival and received *no insight whatsoever* on the fortunes of our respective businesses. Did they advise us on growth strategies or help us to make income projections? No. All they saw were two women with giant holes in their lives. We were without men, which required immediate Wiccan attention.

Once back in Boston, Linda and I stopped in at the hotel bar to discuss our respective fates over a cocktail. We were pondering whether to have a second (or was it a third) drink when the quintessential *elsewhere man* walked in and joined us at the bar.

"Finally," he said in a perfect English accent. "I have been to every bar in Boston trying to find beautiful women in this city, and here you both are!"

It was a trite pick-up line, but it worked. We were enchanted.

I couldn't take my eyes off his perfect teeth as he ordered us a round of cocktails, and was impressed when he specified a top-shelf vodka without my prompting. This *elsewhere man* was exactly what Linda, me, and – well, frankly – every woman is looking for: tall, dark and handsome; rich, fun, smart, sophisticated, and interesting. He looked like Prince Charming. Really. Remember that actor who played Prince Charming in the Cinderella movie and then went on to play Alan Quartermaine on *General Hospital* or *One Life to Live*, or one of those ABC soaps? That's who my first official date with a man from elsewhere looked like. Add to that his English accent, and we're definitely talking Prince Charming here.

Sensing I needed a date more than she did, and now knowing her future husband was patiently awaiting her return to California, Linda excused herself after the one drink and went back to our room. I quickly changed into the little black dress I always pack for just such an occasion, and joined Prince

Charming on his quest to get out and see Boston. And see Boston we did.

After dinner at a trendy new restaurant on the water, it was a madcap night of hopping in cab after cab to visit every bar and nightclub recommended by the hotel concierge. Picture one of those "on-the-town" montages you see in movies or TV shows from the sixties. You know, the couple is running or dancing in the lower frame, looking up occasionally to point and smile, and neon signs and martini glasses appear above them to symbolize all the "hot spots" they have visited.

The Prince was a citizen of the world. He called London home, but spent most of his time in Dubai, Egypt and Africa. I'm not sure what he did for a living, exactly, but it had something to do with finance and Third World economies, and he was in town to attend a symposium at Harvard University the next day. There was a James Bond quality to him, and it made me melt every time he would say, "Where to now, dah-ling?"

Our last stop was an Irish pub where we caught the final few minutes of Karaoke Night. He was still dressed in an expensive suit, looking out-of-place for the first time that evening, but more appealing nonetheless. The prince wanted to show off what he called his "American accent," so he belted out a rendition of John Denver's *Take Me Home, Country Roads*, which sounded a little like Paul McCartney singing with a mouth full of grits. I chose a duet: the love song from Rodgers and Hammerstein's *Cinderella*, which seemed fitting for my date with Prince Charming himself.

Cinderella: Ten minutes ago I met you, you looked up when I came through the door;
Prince: My head started reeling, it gave me the feeling the room had no ceiling or floor...

Two a.m. snuck up on us quickly, and neither of us wanted the night to end. We returned to my hotel and I went to the room I was sharing with Linda to grab a bottle of Chardonnay and two glasses from the mini-bar. She was waiting up for me, and seemed happy – albeit concerned – that all was going well on my dream date. Perhaps thinking I would never return, Linda reminded me as I was walking out the door that I had a plane to catch in the morning, a business back home that would not run itself, and she added final advice to not take the witches' predictions too seriously.

The date with Prince Charming continued in the hotel's courtyard, where we finished the bottle of wine and discussed the challenges of our spanking new long-distance relationship. One thing was as clear as vodka: we did not want to spend another day on Earth without each other. Could I meet him in D.C. in November? Could he spend Christmas in California? Had I ever been to Dubai? How far is San Jose from Dallas? He remembered another symposium at Stanford in the spring. We drank... we kissed... we giggled... and we planned the rest of our lives together.

Soon, it was 3:30 or 4 in the morning, and he was lamenting that he had to be Ivy League in just four hours, and I was realizing I had only three hours before I would need to be going through security at the airport to make my flight. We were slowly accepting reality that our date would have to end.

He grabbed my face, looked into my eyes and said, "I can't wait to see you again." Then he gave me a long, passionate, cinematic kiss that lasted for two or three minutes, during which time my dress started falling off my shoulders and naked logic was beginning to control my thinking. Ignoring Linda's final advisory, I questioned the need to go home at all. *My head started reeling, it gave me the feeling...* then he leaned forward for what I thought was another kiss, but instead chomped down on my lower lip. He bit me.

"Ouch" I said, because it really hurt.

"I am so sorry, dah-ling. I just want to eat you up and I got carried away," he explained breathlessly.

We laughed at that, hugged goodbye, and I returned to my room in tears. (Partly because I had just lost my prince, but mostly because my lower lip was really starting to hurt.) As soon as I put the card key in the door of our hotel room, Linda turned on the light and sat up in bed. And then she screamed. In the mirror across from the front door I saw what she was screaming about. My lip had already swollen to about three times its normal size in the elevator ride to our room on the 21st floor. Blood was seeping out of my mouth and trickling down my chin and neck, and the area around my lower lip was starting to turn blackish-blue.

Linda asked if she should call the police. I said it wasn't necessary and then I started to make excuses.

"He didn't *bean* to do this."

"I had a *gweat* time, *weally*."

"He just got *cay-weed* away."

A few hours later at the airport the swelling had gone down a little, my speech improved a bit, but the bruise was starting to show the detail of teeth marks. Make-up didn't have much of a masking effect, and I finally just gave up and prayed I would not see anyone I knew on the flight home.

I was no longer making excuses for the prince, but instead saying things to myself like:

I can't believe the jerk bit me!

Why did that crazy Brit do this to me?

Carried away, my ass, he's a goddamn vampire!

Unfortunately, I was speaking aloud to the point that I was starting to look like one of those schizophrenic street people who get angry at mailboxes.

There was absolutely no hiding or disguising the fact that someone had bitten me. I couldn't say it was an animal, because the teeth indentations were markedly human. After a few days I was resigned to the only explanation that worked under the circumstances, and it was the truth: "I went out with a man who seemed nice, but then he bit me."

No one asked me to elaborate.

My friend Vicki determined it was her job to make certain this never happened to me, to Linda, or to anyone in our circle of friends again. Of all my single friends, Vicki has been divorced the longest at 25 plus years, and she is the most pragmatic when it comes to matters of the heart. Perhaps her career as a political consultant has jaded her judgment of people. Many clients she worked hard to elect were disappointing representatives once in office, so she has developed strict rules about whom she will represent, and has equally strict rules governing whom she will date. Vicki is set in her ways about a lot of things, such as her intent to never marry again and her unwillingness to take on clients who have ever been registered Republican.

So every time I meet a man who isn't perfect, and I start to rationalize going out with him anyway, Vicki will say something like: "Some of them DO bite, remember?"

If I argue with her, she will start to describe in detail what I looked like for a week in October.

"Your lip was kind of puffy, and there were these perfect little teeth marks right below your lipstick liner that eventually turned into little teeth-shaped scabs."

Vicki is always right – like when she predicted my marriage ending three months before I got the official "you're great, but I'm leaving" speech. She is also right to continue to remind me of the damage done, because my disdain for the prince ended about the same time my lip returned to normal, and I regularly took his phone calls for about a year. Maintaining a long-distance relationship with the prince had a price – an extra $10 per month to upgrade my cell plan – so I could receive his calls from obscure third-world countries.

Even fun-loving Linda, who actually met the Prince and knew he was gorgeous, thought I was crazy to continue talking to a man who bit me, and to pay for the privilege. So on this subject alone, Vicki and Linda were in rare agreement that the prince needed to remain elsewhere.

I can only say in my defense that those first few months of being single and operating under strict dating rules made me rather starved for male attention. His calls were all I had. For me, it was worth every cent to get a daily, then weekly, then monthly call from James Bond that always started, "How are you, dahling?" and always ended with "Miss you, love." Some days the prince's call would cheer me up, but most of the time I just saw his calls as harmless. He could not bite me over the phone.

The conversations were mostly about getting together again, which I knew would never happen. He would be crossing the Atlantic (or as he put it, "on your continent,") but he never seemed to be closer than Washington D.C. or Mexico City. When I asked if he ever made it to California, his answer was "It's a bloody small continent, dah-lng," which I came to understand meant he expected me to do a little traveling too. (I guess wanting to see an expert on failing economies is a rare example of when it is not good to live in a community with a thriving economy.)

So the relationship with Prince Charming was never going to be more than a *phoner*, which was all I was wanting from him anyway. After a while he realized I was not funded well enough to spend weekends in Dubai, and the phone calls stopped.

My lower lip healed and the teeth marks left no permanent scars, which is kind of a shame really. With no physical evidence to remind me, I have only my memory to recall the perfect evening I spent with the perfect man from elsewhere. And I have to rely on my friends to remind me that Prince Charming *bites.*

6

Hot, Hungry and Hammered

My quest to date only men from elsewhere continued through my first year sans-husband. I found some, but very few. There was a business coach from Los Angeles who stopped me on the street one day to ask for directions and then offered to buy me dinner. He said he was in San Jose three days out of every month and we arranged to continue dating. A month later, it became apparent this man from the City of Angels was no angel; he was married. Stan from Ohio told me he was married, but I had dinner with him anyway because... I was hungry, I was starved for male companionship and, well, I didn't know his wife. I also started seeing a man from Denver pretty regularly, but I'll get to him later in my story.

Dates were few and far between in that first year, but I held fast to my strict rules and stayed off the Internet. I could easily have had three or four dates a week if I were still trolling on-line, so the *numbers* were definitely more favorable in the Internet dating pond than on dry land. (You just need to keep their names straight and have more than one lucky blouse.)

One day my friend Molly pointed out that my left hand was still adorned with gems and metal unbefitting a single person.

"Moving your diamond ring to the middle finger of your left hand scares off men who won't take the time to distinguish between two contiguous fingers on the same hand," she said with authority.

"I thought about not wearing it at all," I said, "but I am so used to having it on."

"Absolutely wear the ring," she added. "Wear all your rings!"

To make it extremely obvious I was single, she suggested I wear absolutely no jewelry on the left hand or wrist, and load up my right hand with rings and bangles to show the world I was really, really loved at one time, and probably good in bed too.

I was attending every party I was invited to, and meeting friends for cocktails several nights a week, which was turning me into a heavy drinker, but not a heavy dater. It wasn't until I took Molly's advice and loaded up my right hand with all my wedding rings (the universal sign of a three-time loser, or a very bad wife) that my luck changed. I was at an office-warming party for one of my clients, sporting my newly naked left hand, when a good-looking man about my age sauntered over and introduced himself as Tim. He had just relocated to a job in San Francisco from Kansas City, and had settled in San Jose because he didn't want to be labeled as Gay. Homophobia aside, Tim was a perfect candidate. He didn't work downtown, didn't know a soul in San Jose, didn't work out at my club, and had only a loose tie to my work, through his connection to one client. (Tim was my client's new auditor, a responsibility that changes every year to comply with Sarbanes-Oxley tax regulations on corporations.) Most importantly, he was single, he was incredibly good looking, and he asked for my phone number. We arranged a dinner date for the next Saturday.

It was late spring and northern California was in the midst of a heat wave. The temperature was expected to reach triple digits again the Saturday of my date with Tim. I was planning to while the day away poolside with a book I was eager to read and work on my tan. I had just put on a bikini and poured a tall glass of iced tea when the phone rang.

The call was from the woman who regularly cleaned my vacation rental, calling to say a family emergency would prevent her from meeting her responsibility that day. I called two possible alternates, but neither was available to clean in the tight window between 11 a.m. and 3 p.m. on the hottest day of the year. I quickly surmised that my plans for the day had changed. There was no choice but to drive two and-a-half hours to the house at Lake Nacimiento myself to clean up after a vacationing family, and to prep the house for eight fishermen arriving that afternoon. I put on shorts and a tank top over my swimsuit, re-poured my beverage into a travel mug, and was southbound on Highway 101 within minutes.

I was certain I could accomplish this task and still make it home on time for my dinner date. I called Tim to tell him about my change of plans, and promised to call him from the road to confirm the pick-up time for dinner. He mentioned that it was going to be a hot day and suggested a couple restaurants he knew of that had outdoor dining. Both sounded delicious to me on my empty stomach, so I left the decision of where we would eat in his seemingly capable hands.

I arrived at the lakehouse around noon, and knew this was going to be a tough job. Melted fruit snacks covered the concrete staircase leading to the front door, having been stepped in and smeared around. Sticky stairs turned out to be the least of my worries. The children who had occupied my house for the last week were clearly undisciplined – or perhaps their vacationing parents were just not in the mood for keeping the little ones out of mischief that week. The contents of closets and cabinets were strewn about, including every board game from the game closet. I spent the first hour picking up Monopoly money and Scrabble tiles and arranging them back in their boxes; both of which I found flattened under one of the beds and had to tape back together to re-form as square containers.

Everything in the house was sticky, and the increasing heat was making it worse.

The beautiful view of the lake was not the sight to behold it usually was. The blue water was beckoning me to jump in and soon became a badgering taunt, annoying in its reckless disregard for the many chores needing to be done. I closed all the drapes, sunk into a foul mood, and started fantasizing about doing evil things to adorable toddlers to keep my mind off the mess. I still hadn't eaten anything that day, and was not of right mind.

I was still cleaning the house when the fishermen arrived on time. Explaining my predicament, I promised a partial refund on their day's rental if they would please give me just one more hour. They obliged.

It was almost 5:00 p.m. before I was headed northbound on Highway 101 and I called Tim from the car. We had loosely planned on dinner at 7 and he was to pick me up at 6:30. I would need more time to get home, shower and dress, and asked if we could make it a later dinner – say eight-ish?

Tim had a better idea. With the temperature at 101 degrees – and every indication it was going to be a rare, warm evening in San Jose – he suggested we opt for a more casual evening by the pool. "I can go to Whole Foods and buy us some gourmet salads and a bottle of Pinot Grigio," he said, "and we could picnic by my pool."

This sounded like a better plan to me, considering I was hot, hungry, and longing to be immersed in water of any kind. I was still wearing my bathing suit and dressed appropriately for a picnic, eliminating the need to go home first to shower and change clothes. So I drove straight from my cleaning duties to his place, stopping at a gas station along the way to give myself a quick paper-towel and Purell™ bath in the restroom sink and to apply make-up from my purse.

I hadn't eaten a thing all day, and the hunger pangs were starting to cloud my brain. This date with Tim would be my first evening out with a man in months, and I was too hot and hungry to notice the fruit snacks melted on the soles of my sandals and that my hair smelled like PineSol™. I found his home easily, with my stomach as my navigator along with the crudely drawn map he had scrawled on a cocktail napkin when we met.

Tim was wearing swim trunks and no shirt when he came to the door, and his wet hair indicated he had just gotten out of the pool. He looked different half-dressed and wet than he did when I met him three days earlier. *Was he better looking in a business suit, or was I just so excited about meeting a single, age-appropriate man who seemed interested in me that I made him better looking in my head?* Perhaps, but it didn't matter at the time. I needed to eat.

Tim showed me to the backyard where the only sign of a picnic was an inexpensive bottle of Chardonnay on a side table with two plastic cups. The wine was warm, so he added ice, which did little to cool the wine to a drinkable temperature in this heat and did nothing to make the wine taste like vodka, which is my beverage of choice.

Here I was in a skimpy bathing suit, drinking warm and watered-down pedestrian wine with a not-terribly-attractive man when it dawned on me that I was too drunk to care. I had no food in my stomach to absorb the alcohol, and a thirst so great it should have been quenched with water and not wine. This combination of variables was lethally intoxicating.

Normally alcohol would make me flirty and talkative, but something about Tim – his backyard and the smell of disinfectant that had gotten in my nose – was having the opposite effect. I just wanted to eat and then leave.

I lost track of how many times Tim went back in the house to replenish the wine and ice, but each time he did I hoped to see him return with a basket of food, to no avail. It was close to 9:30 now and he made no motion toward the kitchen and no mention of salads in the refrigerator. My stomach was growling loudly and Tim responded by turning up the volume on his portable I-Pod player.

"I'm hungry," I said finally. "Can we have our salads now?"

Tim looked at me with the glazed-over, disinterested eyes of someone who had spent an entire day drinking warm wine in the hot sun. He was becoming more unattractive every minute. "Maybe with some crackers?" I added.

"I couldn't even imagine eating on a hot day like today," he said, "so I never even bothered to go to Whole Foods." It was then that I realized he was drunk. Could it be that Tim had spent the entire day drinking warm wine by the pool? That would explain why the chilled bottles any self-respecting wine drinker would keep in the refrigerator at all times were gone. If my assumption was correct, I wondered if he even knew I was here.

I stared at him for a little while, trying to craft an appropriate response to this ugly drunk man who had lured me into his backyard under the false pretense of food and had just informed me that I was not going to be fed. The wine had dulled my wit or perhaps it was low levels of naked logic for the bikini I was wearing in a strange man's backyard, but I could not come up with a pithy retort. So I just stood up and headed toward the door.

On my way out I muttered about something very important needing my immediate attention at home and said I would take a rain check on our dinner date. (The only thing that needed immediate attention at my home was the microwave oven in which I would be heating a frozen dinner soon, and the rain check was not going to be cashed in my lifetime.) It really didn't matter what I had said. It only mattered that I got out of there and home to my refrigerator as quickly as possible.

I was still hot and hungry, and – thanks to the cheap wine sloshing around my empty stomach – I was hammered too. I far exceeded the legal limit of alcohol in my system to drive myself home, but the hunger pangs were strong and persistent in convincing me to cast aside my law-abiding ways. I was hot, I was hungry, I was hammered, and there were fruit snacks melted to the soles of my sandals. Convincing myself this was a good defense if I were to find myself facing criminal charges, I drove home.

I was finishing my third *Weight Watchers* frozen dinner in my air-conditioned fish bowl when my phone rang.

"Hello dah-ling." It was Prince Charming calling from someplace in Africa.

I sunk into a comfortable chair and proceeded to tell the man who bit me the story of the man who invited me to dinner and didn't feed me. I am not sure if I would categorize that as the lowest moment in my first year as a single person, but it was definitely one of the most surreal.

7

Garth Brooks, Bad Art and Botox

I have never been much of a crier. I cry when it's appropriate, like when someone dies who is close to me, but that has only happened once in my 50 years. My parents are both alive, and the only two grandparents I knew lived long enough for their passing to be more a celebration of a life well lived than cause for grief.

Diane is someone I think about a lot now that I am single. She was 10 years older than me when we were coworkers and close friends. Her husband had left her for a woman he met on the Internet shortly before her 50th birthday, which was still a novel way to lose your husband back then. While I tried to support her through the difficulties of being a single mom, I couldn't really relate to her challenges because I was a happily married 40 year-old when we became friends.

Diane died of breast cancer at 56 years old - exactly five years after the day they detected a lump in a routine mammogram. She returned to work after double mastectomy surgery in just two days, wearing the fuzzy pink slippers and hospital bracelet that became her wardrobe signature through six months of chemotherapy. We both wore pink survivor ribbons every day for the next five years, and we believed.

She went home with a bad cough one Tuesday, and died two weeks later on Veteran's Day. I didn't cry. I was too busy tending to her family, planning a memorial service, writing her eulogy, and making a video montage of her life.

I went through her vast country music collection to find a song to accompany the montage video, knowing Diane would turn over in her grave if I used something from my own CD collection as the sound-track of her life. (My dislike of country music, and preference for rock, was fodder for a lot of senseless bickering between us.) I listened to everything from Clint to Reba to Patsy and more, all the while sensing Diane laughing her ass off that her passing was forcing me to become immersed in country music.

My brother-in-law is a huge country music fan, and I eventually called him for help. He answered without hesitation: *The Dance*, by Garth Brooks.

I found the song easy enough, listened to a few chords, and took the CD. It's a simple song about having no regrets after the end of a long relationship, but it struck me at the time as the saddest lyric I had ever heard when I interpreted it as a song about the end of a life and not just a relationship.

While listening to Garth sing *The Dance* over and over again to put the audio and video together, my crying became incessant.

I cried for lost beauty as I went through photos from her days as a model.

I cried for her parents who did not expect to bury a child.

I cried for Diane's 16-year-old son who, like me, remained stoic through the process; although, like me, probably found a song, or a sound, or a household object made him cry when no one was looking.

I cried for knowing she had recently reconnected with a childhood crush at a class reunion, yet died single.

I cried for the "Five Years Without Cancer" celebration party we were planning, because it turned out to be her memorial service.

I cried clutching the icon of Diane's battle: a little green army man made into a crude necklace to symbolize the war against cancer which was waged on Veteran's Day; and I cried for the irony that she died in that war on Veteran's Day too.

I cried for all the women wearing pink survivor ribbons with such optimism, because I no longer believed, and was scared for us all.

Mostly I cried because it hurts to have your right arm cut off, and I've always been a baby for pain. For weeks, I would walk home from work having done my easy job and Diane's harder job in fear that I hadn't appreciated her enough for doing the heavy lifting when she was alive.

That was five years ago, and all those feelings come back to me every time I hear that damn song. Just the first few bars are enough, and even an instrumental version played over the *Muzak™* system at the mall will do the trick.

A few months ago, I agreed to be someone's date to the wedding of a couple I had never met. At the reception, the selection of music left no question as to the musical preferences of the bride and groom. *Surely they won't play a song about the end of a relationship at a wedding* I hoped, to no avail, because they did. I heard the first bar of the song, and knew I was in trouble. I dragged my platonic male companion to the dance floor, buried my face in his shoulder, and left most of my eye makeup on his clean, white shirt.

I could see people looking at us, and I'm sure they imagined drama unfolding in our not-a-relationship. My date kept saying he understood that I had been through a lot, and I was too choked up to tell him my tears had nothing to do with my recently failed marriage.

That was seven months after my husband moved out, and it was the first time I had cried. The first time I cried.

The next crying episode happened only two months later at the lakehouse my soon-to-be-ex and I still own together. Freshly hung on a prominent living room wall were two very large acrylic paintings: a diptych of a fly fisherman in different poses on the same Snake River bend. The paintings were in a crude, expressionist style and the ornate frames finished in antique gold; clearly not in theme with the folksy-yet-contemporary Swedish country motif I had worked so hard to achieve in this room. And I had never seen a fly fisherman on Lake Nacimiento, since it's a reservoir and much too deep to stand in wearing waders.

My first reaction to the new living room décor was to throw my keys at them, which was only slightly cathartic. Next the armload of towels I was carrying were cast in the general direction of the paintings, but lacked the dramatic effect of the keys when they fell only a few feet from where I was standing and remained folded. Since throwing things failed to make me feel better, I dropped to the living room floor and cried the way a spoiled toddler might, by occasionally beating the floor with my fist.

In the 10 years we had owned the house at Lake Nacimiento, my husband and I operated under an unwritten agreement to which the inside of the house was my exclusive purview and everything on the outside was his. Now there was someone else looking at the inside of my house with tastes, opinions and artist friends of her own.

Somehow it hadn't hit me that I would be sharing my vacation home with another woman. I understood that my soon-to-be-ex and I were hanging on to the asset and it seemed only natural, and very practical, to do so. I had no issues with the new girlfriend being at the house per se', but I hadn't thought through the challenges of our arrangement and how it would be impacted by our new status. He will someday become another family unit, and perhaps I will end up in another family unit, and somehow we two family units – who were not friends and would never be in this house together – would have to consult each other on home improvement decisions. Why this hadn't occurred to me before that moment, I don't know.

Is that why I was crying? Or was it the subject matter of the paintings – and a histrionic surrender to my certain fate as a 50-year-old fisherman? There *I* stand, alone in a river wearing waist-high waders and lashing wildly at the current with a rod and a reel. They were two nearly identical images of the same scene. In one painting the fisherman is casting; his arm stretched high in the air, the line in a perfect arc over his head. In the second he is reeling in a fish, which you can see from the tautness of the line and the animated way in which he leans backwards, holding the reel near his chest with his elbows tight. The river is depicted as lines of blue, brown and grey, while dots of white and yellow make dapples of sunlight on the water's surface. The paintings taunted me like evil twins and I wondered whether the artist had captured two moments in the same day, or two moments in a life-time of fishing?

Whatever deep-seated emotional anguish those paintings resurrected in me at the time went away as soon as I moved the fisherman paintings from the living room to a back bedroom, and my crying stopped. Later, I realized my breakdown had nothing to do with mid-life dating, my failed marriage, or Diane. I just didn't like the way the paintings clashed with the couch.

Coincidentally, the woman who became my soon-to-be-ex-husband's girlfriend, and presumably hung the paintings, was someone Diane knew. I only know of the connection because I remember Diane telling me once that she had sold her hot tub to the same woman. One day Travis told me he had earned money on a Saturday helping my soon-to-be-ex-husband make repairs to his new girlfriend's old hot tub. I remembered then soaking in that hot tub when it was Diane's, and thought it a small world to know the same vessel in which girlfriends huddled to talk about men had become a romantic place for one of those men to nourish a fledgling relationship.

The hot tub at our lakehouse used to be in Vicki's back yard, and I imagine my soon-to-be-ex has spent many evenings soaking up romance in our hot tub since becoming single. I can't dwell on those things, so I try to focus on my list of things to do. The hot tub needs to be replaced this year, and my friend Molly has already offered to give me hers. In Northern California, hot tubs are like husbands. Everyone has one, you enjoy it a lot when it's new, and they tend to end up in someone else's backyard eventually. (Faulty plumbing can become a nuisance after a while, but there's always someone who can get an old tub hot enough to enjoy a couple years of soaking for the price of a flatbed truck rental and a small crew.)

The last time I soaked in the lakehouse hot tub was the night after I got my first Botox injections. As soon as the steamy water hit my face I remembered that this was on the list of forbidden activities they handed me on my way out the door. I wasn't happy to get the instructions because I misunderstood what they said about it being a simple procedure with no "down time." You can't soak in a hot tub, drink alcohol, or be in the sun for at least 24 hours after getting Botox injections, which to me means 24 hours of avoiding the activities I associate with "down time."

I was always planning to be one of those women who age gracefully. Diane laughed at me once when I said that, and pointed out that I was barely middle age and happily married. Diane always knew my future, at ten years my senior. Sure enough, when my friend and co-worker Sandy came running into my office one day not too long ago with an exciting offer of two-for-one Botox at our neighborhood Med Spa, I jumped at the chance. I reminded myself that Botox was known to cure migraines, and rationalized the procedure as being preventive and not restorative, therefore not counting as a cosmetic procedure.

We made an appointment for the next week, and heartily agreed when they asked if we wanted to get our injections together. Sandy went first, and the procedure appeared to be quick and painless, as advertised. Her daughter called, as they were about to start on me, so she stepped out into the hallway to take the call. When Sandy returned she looked at me, shocked, and said, "Are YOU crying???"

I was crying, like a little baby; it hurt so much. Or did it hurt? Was I crying because they had stuck a pretty heavy gauge needle into my forehead and it was starting to bleed? Or was I crying because I had lost the will to age gracefully? Was a face-lift next? Collagen injected in my lips? Would I know where to draw the line, or was I stepping into that dangerous territory women my age refer to as "work," as in "she's had work done." This was beyond work in my mind, because I would pull an eight-hour shift doing the worst job in the world before I would have a needle stuck in my head for five seconds again.

Of course I said that the last time I got my eyebrows waxed, and I still show up for my monthly appointment without fail. What is it they say about childbirth? If women had a memory for pain, no one would have brothers or sisters. Vanity will win out over pain every time; as will romance, by the way, because I surely would have allowed myself to be bitten again for another enchanted evening with Prince Charming.

After her mastectomy, Diane underwent reconstructive surgery resulting in a massive infection and two weeks in ICU. Weeks later she told me she had survived the cancer, but almost succumbed to the vanity procedure. Still she wore an itchy wig to cover her hairless skull during six months of painful chemotherapy, for vanity again. She cried a lot, and had every right to.

I guess shedding a few tears here and there is okay for good reason. Until something rocks my world that is really worth crying about (and it wasn't turning 50 or even my husband walking out,) one Garth Brooks song, art that doesn't match the room, and anything that just really, really hurts are good enough reasons for me.

8
The Tail Club

The Tail Club started six or seven years ago, before I was single, shortly after my husband entered into his second midlife crisis and started a rock band. The band was cute at first, but became not so funny anymore when they started getting gigs, which lead to getting publicity. Soon he was introducing himself to new acquaintances as the drummer in a "hot" new band, and not by his real, full-time profession as my business partner, or as my husband.

Every Monday night the band would rehearse, and I got into the habit of meeting Vicki at *The Grill on The Alley* for drinks. One night our newly divorced friend Kathy joined us, and then Molly – who was the lead singer in my husband's band until the guys got too serious – decided she would rather drink with us than make music with them. Soon we had formed what we loosely called The Ladies Monday Night Drinking Club.

Several more women joined in the weekly gabfest, and the need to shorten the name to something that would fit in a calendar became apparent to Kathy, who was the managing partner of a prominent law firm and feared her administrative assistant was beginning to suspect she was an alcoholic for scribbling the word "drinking" in her calendar every Monday. Trish, who is happily married and the CFO of a small software company, suggested we call it the Ladies Wine Club, since wine drinking is more upscale and respectable, and it's her beverage of choice. Vicki pointed out that adding "Ladies" to the word "Wine," sounded like a PMS support group, and that name was unanimously abandoned. Besides, our signature drink was not wine, but anything with a splash of cranberry juice to promote vaginal health. (Vodka/diet tonic with a splash o' cran is my drink of choice.) My contribution to the debate was noting a preference for the term "cocktail" over "drink" because I think it sounds more retro-festive.

So the Club was called the Ladies Monday Night Cocktail Club for a few Mondays, until we realized that dropping "cock" from cocktail would altogether eliminate the need for a gender qualifier, and the name could be shorter yet.

The Monday Night Tail Club (or MNTC in my calendar) became just The Tail Club about the same time it became a gathering place for single fishermen, and we started meeting on multiple nights of the week. There are still a few married women in the group (Kathy, for one, remarried around the same time I became single,) but mostly they attend to live vicariously through the girls in the pond.

Mary was attending regularly for a year or so, and then stopped. Two years later she resumed attending religiously, when her husband retired and she needed to get away. Lee comes every third Monday, when her husband has a Board meeting; Suzanne comes in the summer months when *The Bachelor* goes into reruns; and Linda – who has been living in her condo at the beach since the naked incident – only attends when she has a late afternoon meeting in downtown San Jose. And then there's the other Cathy – Cathy with a "C" – who was married when we started to meet, but became a regular when she left her husband, which coincidentally happened on the anniversary of my marriage ending the year before.

Lisa, the publisher of a trade publication serving the on-line gaming industry, and an early member of the Tail Club, has made it to middle age without a single trip down the aisle. She was the first to drop a line in the water, and she did so without so much as a hint of what was to come.

"Does anyone here want to go with me on a date?" Lisa said one Monday night without sitting down to join us.

"Why would we want to go with you on a date?" asked Molly, who was in the middle of telling us the dramatic, true story of her two-year relationship ending over the weekend.

Lisa explained this wasn't a real date, but an Internet date. She was meeting for the first time someone she had become acquainted with on a website called *Plenty of Fish*, and he was waiting for her at a popular brewpub down the street. Then she showed us his picture on her smart phone, which was intriguing, because he was actually kind of cute. This was so like Lisa to shift the paradigm of our little club with no drama or fanfare, much like she would not volunteer major news – like that she had started a new business, or that she had ended a long relationship – unless specifically asked. Sharing major life events was the whole point of the club, but Lisa didn't share anything about herself, unless it was obvious like a drastic new hairstyle, or it was drawn out of her through a set of very pointed questions.

One Monday, for example, someone asked Lisa how her boyfriend Greg was, and she said that she didn't know. More probing revealed that Greg had moved out several months earlier. Only when asked for details did she tell of the note she found and all his belongings gone when she returned from a weeklong Publisher's Conference months before. It seems she had left town without telling him, which she said was hard for her to remember to do after living alone for so long. It was unclear, therefore, whether Greg had left Lisa or assumed she had abandoned him. We will never know for sure, because – in sharp contrast to all other members of the Tail Club – getting information out of Lisa was like pushing a boulder uphill.

It turns out Lisa had been fishing the Internet for a while, but this fish named Seth was the first she felt compelled to meet in person. It seems that Seth and Lisa actually shared an interest in the work of poet Charles Bukowski and we were in shock that she could have found a man who could even spell Bukowski, let alone appreciate poetry, on a website named after a cliché'.

NANCI WILLIAMS

I told Lisa she was being set-up by a con artist, and I feared it to be true, because it was not possible that someone who loves poetry and looks like a regular person could be found on the Internet. I mentioned that my sister had been meeting some very odd men on the very same site, and did not disclose my own short voyage across the *Plenty of Fish* pond about eight months earlier.

Lisa heeded my warning with a smile, and headed to her date with Molly tagging along. Her capacity as Lisa's bodyguard was secondary to her role as the Tail Club's spy, and Molly reported back to us promptly. She said this fish named Seth seemed normal; looked like his picture; and that she had left Seth and Lisa in an animated conversation about hyperboles, consonance and assonance.

It was several months before we saw Lisa again and learned that Seth had moved in with her only a week after that initial meeting and that they had recently bought a dog.

Molly was so enthused about Lisa's great catch that she went on-line that night and became a fisherman. The best way to get over a man is to get under a man, after all, and Molly really needed to get over a man.

By the next Tail Club meeting, Molly had been on three coffee dates and had met at least one very delicious and two not-so-stinky fish. Vicki was hooked, and had her line in the water the next night. Linda gave the others about a week to be her guinea fish before jumping in the pond herself.

With all my single friends now fishing, going back

to the *Plenty of Fish* pond was the only alternative to becoming very, very lonely, so I re-set my hook. Then I convinced my recently separated business partner and best non-girlfriend Mike to jump in the pond, partly so he could tell us how well our lures were working from the point-of-view of a fish. Mike was useless in that capacity, however, because he blocked women of our advanced age; he swims in the exclusive 35-and-under pond.

Vicki's first date was a keeper, but she kept fishing anyway. Mitch was great, and their date went late into the evening. So I was a little surprised to see HER Mitch in MY livewell the next day, but I was still new to the sport of fishing, and didn't yet know this was common in the pond.

"Didn't you just go out with my best friend Vicki?" I asked him in an email. "Yes, and I had a very good time," he responded. "I really like Vicki."

Then why are you emailing me? I thought, but didn't reply. Vicki took the news about Mitch in stride, because she already had two more coffee dates with seemingly cute fish set up for the next week.

Always willing to jump on an airliner to chase a dream, Linda did not limit her fishing to our little pond, but chose to troll the entire country. Therefore, her fishing escapades took her to a new city every weekend, and we didn't see Linda for several Mondays. When we did, she had a stringer of great catches and was giddy to report on more action during her short period of time in the pond than she had in the previous 15 years of being single on dry land.

This time in the pond was better for me emotionally, because I was no longer fishing alone. My first date was a doctor and the second was a lawyer, and both were charming fish who – believe it or not – were better looking in person than in their pictures. Imagine that. Most of the fish seem to just snap a picture of themselves on their phone or grab something from their last vacation album, so there's no retouching or professional trickery to the profile photos of fish. (Women are a little better at this.)

Except for Mike, we were all experiencing "nothing but net" in the first couple weeks in the pond. The lone fish in my circle of fishing buddies took a little longer to figure out the difference between a live wiggly worm and a plastic lure in the early days. Mike was stood up not once, not twice, but three times on coffee dates. As I meet more fish, I have started asking them about this, and it seems getting stood up is rather common for fish, but I have yet to hear a woman report a no-show dating experience. I have never found women to be flakier and less reliable than men in the workplace or in life, leading me to believe that men like Mike are less able to recognize the telltale signs in a profile which indicate their prospect was not committed to the sport. I look for things like how long they were in their last relationship, or how often they are on-line. Those few facts tell me if someone has a life outside of the pond, for one, and whether they are capable of being in a relationship. Mike didn't look at any of those things, and most men don't. It seems they look only at the photo, and probably deserve to be stood up once in a while.

The five of us in the pond range in age from the late 40s to late 50s, with Lisa at the lowest and Vicki at the highest end of the spectrum. The age variance means we seldom run into the same fish – as strange as that sounds in this small pond, and Mitch being one exception – because fish are very selective about the age of the worms they will bite. If they are 45, they list their age range as 30 to 46. If they are 50, the acceptable age range will be 35 to 51. So, while women prefer to date men close to their own age, men consider women 15 years younger to be acceptable, but more than a year older is not to be. (*Minnows* – defined as anyone young enough for us to have given birth to – are an exception to this rule, thanks to the fairly recent "cougar" phenomenon being practiced mostly in Hollywood.)

Other than issues of age, dating at 50-something is much the same as dating at 20-something except the number of variables is significantly greater. Does he have any hair? His own teeth? Does he still work, or is he retired? (Since we all work, we can't imagine being in a relationship with someone who has no place to go every day.) What someone does for a living is important to our group, since we all have good jobs. Other lifestyle elements such as golf handicap, geographic location, willingness to travel, and compatible sched-ules are major considerations as well.

Golf handicap is important to Molly, because the man she was getting over was a scratch golfer, and he needed replacing on the links and in her bed. Lisa cares about reading habits, Linda cares about workout habits, and Vicki is completely unwilling to date a Republican. What a man does for a living is not as important to me, but we will have nothing to talk about if he is not good at whatever it is he does. Phrases like "my job is not who I am" in a profile hint at a fish who is not obsessive about his work, like I am, which will result in his immediate release.

I didn't consider any of these factors when I was in my twenties. Looks were all that mattered, followed closely by ability to pay for dinner at a fast-food restaurant, and a sense of humor. Those traits were present in about 30 to 40 percent of age appropriate men in those days. We were all too young to have had careers that mattered; everyone had their hair and their teeth; everyone was liberal and didn't have time to read; and beer bellies were just barely starting to sprout at twenty-something. We didn't have to worry about details like his visitation schedule with his kids, or whether he is available to relocate, because no one had kids yet and everyone lived in temporary housing.

Remember when you could date someone for a couple of weeks, and then start looking for an apartment together? Unless you are limiting your prospects to the homeless population, all the men you will meet at mid-life are firmly planted in the dream home they purchased after the wife got the family home, or in the condo near the kids' school where he intends to stay until Bob Junior graduates from college in eight years or so.

I love my fishbowl, and he loves his condo, so moving in together is probably not in the cards. Which is fine, because we get pretty set in our ways at this age as well. We wake up at 4 a.m. to go to the gym, or we watch television in bed until we fall asleep, and can't fall asleep without it. By 50-something we have developed habits that are hard to break and harder to live with. Finding a suitable partner to share our world, who has a compatible profession, shared interests, votes right, kids who are grown, and is finished battling his ex-wife for the big house *is hard*. And finding someone who will love my menagerie of pets as much as I do, has his own pets who I could love and my pets could tolerate, and who undoubtedly has eccentricities and habits he also cannot change and I could tolerate is *really, really hard.*

So the Tail Club fishing reports are usually about wonderful catches, and the not-so-wonderful lifestyle traits that make every wonderful fish unsuitable. Even Lisa eventually returned to the Tail Club to lament that perfect, poetry-loving Seth was wishing to leave her downtown condo for a house in the suburbs. The suburbs are out of the question for ALL of the Tail Club members, so this is simply a deal-breaker. So whether Seth will choose Lisa and an urban lifestyle, or whether Lisa will choose love and poetry in the land of Little League and strip malls has yet to be definitively determined.

I couldn't help but notice that Seth is back in the pond, and it appears that Lisa is back in the Tail Club, so which of them stays at home with their dog is not certain. On a long ago visit to an animal shelter, I noted that many of the surrendered pups were listed as being

6 to 10 months old, which I found curious at the time. I get it now. These poor animals were probably the innocent victims of fishing accidents.

9

A Fish Named Andy

One of my happily married girlfriends told me she keeps a Match.com profile active, just because she's curious. I guess a lot of us who married long before the Internet changed the dating world are curious to know how our lives might have turned out differently if a tool of this magnitude had been available to help us find a soul mate instead of, well, just vodka and push-up bras.

So I would like to come clean about something: My *very* first foray into Internet dating was a few years ago, when I was still married.

I registered on Match.com as a 45-year-old man named Andy Bingham, so I could voyeuristically spy on my recently divorced girlfriend Cindy, who was dating up to eight men per week on the site. Cindy was so prolific and so popular on Match.com that she was once invited to be the guest on a radio call-in show on the subject of on-line dating.

My Andy tried several times to get in touch with Cindy on Match.com, but she had blocked users without photos from contacting her, or even from seeing her profile. Smart girl, I thought, and I was done.

The mad-matching minions at Match.com, however, were not done and were not going to rest until Andy got a date. They were aggressive in their pursuit of a match for Andy, and at one second past midnight every single night for several months they emailed me a photo and brief summary of women they thought my Andy would like.

Therefore, the very first email I received every day was from the Match-minions. Photos of age-appropriate women with captions like, "Wildcat in bed, pussycat in your arms," "I have been waiting for YOU," "Lonely lady looking for love," and... well, you get the gist. It altered my perception of ALL women to experience the mating behavior of my female cohorts from this unique perspective from inside the pond. I felt guilty. I felt like a traitor.

The Andy I described was average in every way, and there was no photo accompanying his profile; so one would naturally assume he was less than attractive. Yet women were throwing themselves at him shamelessly, with the help of the Match-minions. It was a hard thing for me to see as a married woman – especially when someone I knew was sent for Andy's consideration.

One person I recognized showed up with the heading "Try Me!" I got the double entendre in her headline because I know Marion's a lawyer/litigator by profession. Would others get it? Did she intend to make word play, or was she advertising herself like a Hickory Farms cheese log? I shuddered at the thought. Her photo was not the handsome head-and-shoulders portrait she uses on her law firm's website. It was something sexy and flirtatious, and Marion no longer looked like the smart, poised professional I knew her to be.

A self-proclaimed feminist named Jenny, who used to work at our agency, showed up with my morning coffee one day. She wanted Andy to know that her breasts were "real and they were spectacular," to steal Terry Hatcher's line from a somewhat famous Seinfeld episode. *Et tu, Jenny?* Please don't let me believe that you who graduated top of your class at UC Berkeley would pedal your flesh pillows like they were Viagra by spamming guys like Andy. Shame on you!

I half expected to see Valley CEOs like Meg Whitman or Carly Fiorino emailed for Andy's consideration with a headline like "I want to be on top," or "Boss Lady 4-U," but then I remembered the Match-minions. It was not Jenny or Marion spamming me every day, and I'm pretty sure that Meg and Carly are both married. It was those pesky Match-minions! Should I call Andy's prospects and let them know the Match-minions had served them up with my morning bagel that day? They would be mortified. I would be mortified. So I left it alone.

It was partly because of my time as Andy that I was initially pessimistic about Internet dating. That and the fact that my friend Cindy, after four years of prolific fishing, finally caught the man of her dreams and got married. But it took 589 dates for her to find her prince, so I was left to believe the ratio of bad men to good men on-line is not much different than in the real world: 589 to 1.

And Jack just didn't strike me as the big fish I was envisioning for Cindy, who worked the pond more skillfully than any fisherman I have ever known. Her lures were shiny, her bait was fresh, and there was never a day she didn't have a line in the water. Cindy was a true wiggler.

In the real world I would find Jack to be a decent enough human being. One just has very high expectations in a fishing tournament. He is a downtown attorney, which made me wonder why she couldn't have just met him at Starbucks, where there are schools of lawyers and bankers on any given day in this very small pond. She had the Internet – *an entire ocean of fish* – as her hunting ground, but the one she kept was a local guy who looked like my accountant.

Cindy met Jack in December, he proposed on Valentine's Day, and they were married in early May. Since I now know that on-line relationships move at DSL speed, this timing is no longer surprising to me. All the information it takes years to learn about a prospective partner on dry land is detailed in the on-line profile. So it was like their first date was their 10th date, and their second date was their 20th date, and the pressure on Jack to make an honest woman of Cindy after swimming around together for 45 days seems strangely appropriate.

Now that I am fishing, I completely understand why it took Cindy 589 dates to meet Jack. It wasn't that there were 589 bad fish that preceded the one keeper; it was that there were 589 fish, period. As everyone who has worked this pond knows, even a coffee date that goes well is seldom repeated. As soon as I log on to pen my obligatory "Thanks for a great time" note, I am drawn to five new fish in my livewell.

Since I only have a couple free nights per week for fish dating, I have to weigh the pros and cons of catching new fish versus swimming around with the ones in my net. This doesn't happen on dry land, unless you are a contestant on *The Bachelor*. I have never come home from a date in the real world and found five men lined up on my front porch saying, "Would you like to go out for coffee?"

That bounty is not reserved for fine catches such as Cindy. Not-so-attractive Andy met the fish of his dreams, when I finally decided he was ready. I changed his profile one day to read, "sorry ladies, but this fish has been caught," and attached a picture from my second wedding. Eventually, someone reported Andy to the Match-minions and the morning emails stopped. Andy did get one more email, from the advertising agency representing Match.com, asking if he was interested in telling his story in a television commercial for the dating site. I called my second ex-husband to see if he wanted to do the gig with me – which would involve both of us passing for 45-year-olds who looked 28, like in the picture – but his wife nixed the idea, thinking it would confuse their three kids. I'm proud of my Andy for becoming another Match.com success story, even if we're not going to be TV stars.

10
In The Tubes

My *Plenty of Fish* username, "Inthetubes," is in reference to a phrase we started using at the office after the late Ted Stevens, then a United States Senator from the State of Alaska, referred to the Internet as "a series of tubes." It was a big joke here in Silicon Valley, and there were a few weeks when people around here would laughingly say they were sending a file through the "tubes." Anytime email gets backed up, or Internet access slows down, someone in my small advertising agency will yell - "Something's stuck in the tubes," or "Whose turn is it to plunger the tubes?" which is another way to say, "restart the server." Diving into the tubes to join my friends was like re-booting my social life and admitting there was simply not enough time in the real world, or fish on dry land, for me to date recreationally.

My idea of what single life should be was more like Holly Golightly from *Breakfast at Tiffany's*, and less like the whiny single heroines that Diane Keaton always plays in movies these days. Sure, Diane's character always gets her man at the end of the film, but until then she lives a lonely, angst-filled existence. Her friends and family spend the first half of the movie worried about her, which is most definitely not what I want.

On the other hand, Holly Golightly does not get the man. (In the romanticized movie version of *Breakfast at Tiffany's*, Holly does get her man in the end to appease a largely female audience. But I am loyal to the book, wherein the George Peppard character is actually a gay man created in the likeness of the author, Truman Capote, and not someone the heroine would want as a lover.) Capote's Holly didn't need just one man, because men fell like rain from the sky at her feet. She wanted a life, and would only accept a man who came with a life better than the one she was living.

I am mindful of the fact that Holly Golightly was a call girl, but I still envy the hell out of her wit, her independence, her wardrobe, and her social life. And Holly wasn't a sex-for-hire kind of call girl anyway. She was more like your average single girl, by contemporary standards, in that men would buy her things – like jewelry and airline tickets – and give her "powder room change" as she needed it. How is that different from letting men buy me dinner and drinks, give free legal advice, or buy stock at a preferred price in their start-up company? Upon reflection, I am as much of a call girl as Holly, except I don't ask for powder room change every time I use the bathroom.

The Internet offered a better opportunity to be out every night, like Holly Golightly, than my real life did. My first year of being unattached did not include a social life befitting an active, new single person. I didn't even meet, let alone date, many men at all.

I have three partners and four employees at my small advertising agency. My business partners are men, but the newest is 20 years my junior; the other is Mike, who is my best male friend, so he doesn't count; and the third is my soon-to-be-ex husband. Been there, done that. That leaves clients, which is never a good idea; vendors, which is an even worse idea; employees, which is against the law; and men who I may just run into on the street. Two of the three men I dated in the year before I jumped in the tubes were from the latter category: a random man I met standing at a crosswalk, and another who stopped me to ask for directions. Both were from out-of-town, making them oh-so-sought-after *men from elsewhere.*

I do live in a high-rise building, and there are at least three single, heterosexual men in residence that I am aware of. One of them asked me out in the elevator one day, but the idea of dating someone who does not have to go through security to see me is a little daunting. This is especially true if the date doesn't go well, but if it *does* go well I would be in an equally bad position. I need my space, even when I am in a relationship (which goes a long way toward explaining my three failed marriages), so dating someone who can pop in at any time would suffocate me. So once I added neighbors to my "Do Not Date list," and amended my stand on Internet dating, I was back to *elsewhere men* whom I might meet in a crosswalk, but were considerably more plentiful on-line.

I exaggerated my active tendencies in my new on-line dating profile because I wanted to weed out couch potatoes. First I warned nibblers that I was in need of constant stimulation. Then I went on to describe a first date involving jumping out of airplanes together before downing Tequila shots and nightclubbing until closing time. I nixed the idea of sipping wine at sunset.

This second time in the pond I was looking for something completely different from the respectable men I tend to attract and end up marrying. I wanted an active adventurer; someone who could party the night away and never have a hangover; someone who could make me laugh. A cross between James Bond and Will Farrell? Or perhaps there's a version of me with a penis out there? (I like to think that if I were a man I would have a magnificent penis.)

The very first bite I got with my new, improved profile was a message from a psychologist who unscientifically diagnosed me as an adrenaline junkie, and suggested I seek help. In his professional opinion, he said I should not be seeking the kind of man who will enable my bad behavior. Then he asked if I wanted to meet for coffee, but I released him. This head-shrinking fish clearly didn't get me.

The biggest challenge to Internet dating presented itself early on: there is only so much time available for kissing frogs (or fish, in this case), if you want to have a life outside of dating that includes work, friends, hobbies, and family. Fishing can take over your life if you let it. The sheer number of fish on-line is staggering to the uninitiated: just under 2,000 age-appropriate men in San Jose alone. And to think that I had only met three on dry land, and none of them lived anywhere near me.

The Internet livewell is full of prospects. After releasing the obviously unsuitable fish, there are still too many remaining to date in a week. Do I chat with them for a while, or make a meeting quickly to determine whether they are suitable for catch? Some of my fishing buddies say they want to get the meeting over as quickly as possible, while others tell me they like to correspond with a fish for at least a week or two before making a meeting. I did a little of both at first.

My problem is that I can fall in love with someone who writes well and thinks like I do, sight unseen. So there were a couple of instances early on where I was excited about meeting a fish I had been corresponding with for a week. The disappointment I experienced upon discovering they were not nearly as attractive as the picture in my head, was beyond something I could hide. There is nothing more humiliating to me than seeing a look of disappointment on a man's face when I first enter a room. Surely fish can't be so different from me that they don't see this.

I was wrong on the latter part, because men do not interpret subtle facial expressions the way women do. No matter how disappointed I was to meet certain fish, they continued to communicate well beyond the initial meeting – even when I was not communicating back. Interesting the way fish think, and interesting that fish have no ability to sense intuitively that a woman is not interested. I know I should communicate my disinterest clearly and without ambiguity, but I don't like confrontation, and have learned it is just as effective to avoid said fish for a week and they will swim away. (They don't swim away because they get the hint; they swim away because another shiny lure has captured their interest.)

I also find it worth noting that many fish do not like to have on-line conversations for very long, if at all. Quite often responses to my pithy emails simply include a phone number and the words "call me." If I do call, the only thing they have to say is "Where are you now? I have a navigator."

Many fish in the pond don't even have the patience to start with a coffee date. One of my emails from a fish was an invitation to go skiing that weekend.

Hi,

I like the way you look, and I see that you are a skier. I have a cabin in Tahoe, and it's just my kids and me this weekend. I am leaving later today. We can get to know each other on the drive. My name is Ken, and my number is (408) 555-6362.

I love to ski, so I was tempted, but I could not imagine a first date lasting an entire weekend, let alone a weekend with his kids. If I really, really hate him, I am obliged to stay in his company the whole weekend, and I would most likely bond with his kids after two days, even if he were a jerk. My two stepsons got attached to me quickly, and I got attached to them easily, so this has all the trappings of my next failed marriage if I accept this bizarre proposition. I reluctantly declined the invitation to ski free in exchange for playing *mom* for the weekend.

I did meet Ken for coffee a few weeks later, and learned that his 28-year-old daughter and her husband were the "kids" he referred to in his email. Still, I had zero chemistry with Ken, so it was good I didn't spend a weekend with him providing false hope of a future together. It's also good I didn't see his cabin, because real estate is my cocaine, and has a way of clouding my brain. If I liked the cabin, and saw untapped potential, I would have stayed with Ken for as many years as it took for me to remodel and redecorate. Vicki, Molly and I are all *real estate junkies*, in that we get a sense of euphoria when we are buying and fixing houses. Since we lack the funds to buy a house a month, and can only move every other year or so, we cannot get our fix as often as we need it. So we perpetually look at property for sale, and then draw up architectural plans and a financial pro-forma to buy one we like, in the event one of us were to win the lottery within the week.

I could graduate from real estate junkie to real estate whore for the right property, I think. We could open a brothel for real estate whores, and I just know we could get Linda, Lisa and Cathy to join in the action, because real estate is to smart girls what diamonds are to blondes. *First we will need a very large house...*

This is all just a fantasy, of course, because there are no fish in the pond willing to part with real estate for sexual favors. As one man I dated pointed out, everyone in the pond is divorced and most have been divorced recently. That means that everyone lost a house in the not-so-distant past, and is likely living in a small apartment or condo. Fish can get cranky real fast if you even joke about taking real estate away from them. I know this because a fish hung up on me when he mistook an innocent comment I made as a money grab of sorts.

The hang-up was from a fish named John, who sent me one of those emails with just a phone number. I called him, and he said he was busy but would call again now that he had my number. Several days later he did call, but the conversation was a short one. I asked him what he did for a living and he said he invested in real estate. "That's great," I said, "because I love real estate!" He hung up.

John's hang-up rang in my ears for a long while, during which time I collapsed in frustration on the fake grass on my patio. Staring at the greenish blades from that humiliating vantage point gave me the strength I needed to remember that I owned my own fishbowl, had a good career, and didn't need a fish to provide me with shelter. So I raised my arm to the sky – clutching a handful of artificial turf in my fist – and said (into an imagined camera): "With God as my witness, I will never be hung up on again."

It took that movie-screen moment to realize that any communication – telephone, email, or otherwise – was pointless. Coffee dates were the only way to process the fish in my livewell. Surely John would not have run away from me in fear if he had seen the sparkle in my eyes when I said "I love real estate." He would have been dazzled by my bubbly personality (or frightened by my killer abs) and he would have signed over the deed to a house or two right away.

I am better in person, I determined, and would just have to make the time to have coffee with *every* fish who bit on my worm. And I did. The first half of February was spent on fish date after fish date, until Starbucks employees throughout the valley got to know me by name. By Valentine's Day, I achieved a personal best with six bouquets, two boxes of candy, and 16 e-cards.

Finally, I am Holly Golightly.

11
Tournament Rules

Maybe word got out about my degree in sociology, or perhaps it was the many Starbucks employees
I befriended, but after I had been in the pond for a few
months, people started asking me for advice on fishing.
The first thing I tell them is this: men are fish and
women are fishermen. My reason for assigning these
roles is the law of nature: women are natural wigglers
after all, and men tend to wander around without
direction. The theory of naked logic is another reason
for my thinking in this regard, since there are bushy
trees and shrubbery on dry land, in the event of acci-
dental nudity. And fish are naked, while fishermen
wear an absurd amount of clothing for a sport that
takes place on water. Women like to have a special
outfit for every activity, and every single woman I know
has a lucky blouse she wears on dates.

I have had men argue this fact with me. They like
to think of themselves as natural hunters, so the
concept of being hunted doesn't bode well with them.
But the difference between fishing and hunting is the
existence of a lure. A hunter doesn't lure game into the

sight of a rifle: fishermen do. And women have made a science of luring men through provocative clothes, make-up and scents. Like a man, a fish will wander from lure to lure trying to avoid the hook, until one day when he least expects it he has been caught.

Like anyone new to the sport of fishing, women who didn't grow up with a worm farm in their backyard need to learn the proper way to bait a hook. Affix the worm in such a way that it is secure, but leave just a little tail free to wiggle. If you simply pierce the worm once in the center, it will be allowed too much wiggle-room and the fish will be able to eat away at the bait, without coming close to the hook. (See Figure A.) That means no sex on the first date, no cleavage in the profile photo, no phone sex before the first date, and no inquiries as to penis size in your initial contact.

FIGURE A

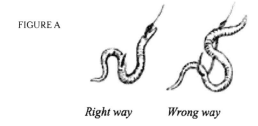

Right way   Wrong way

Many of the fish I dated told me stories of very aggressive sexual behavior from fishermen – like sending nude photos, or suggesting the coffee date take place in their bedroom. Frankly, these women scare away their fish, which is easy to do with fish, and often will cause a feeding frenzy amongst the minnows. I equate these sexually aggressive women to the fishermen who sneak live bait on their hook in a bass tournament, when regulations strictly forbid anything but lures.

I discovered an interesting anecdote that counters the no sex rule, however. I interviewed three fish in the pond as part of my armchair sociological research and ALL three said that *every* woman they went out with had sex with them on the first date. *The COFFEE date, mind you!* And, without exception, each of these women said they had never done anything like that before.

And these women were not bimbos. These were college professors, soccer moms and doctors – all resorting to the high school-like behavior of giving in to their basic instinct, and then pretending it had never happened before to preserve their reputation.

One of the fish I interviewed believed the women who said they had never done this before, and thought himself to be a sexual dynamo that could challenge even the morally chaste of our gender. The other two said they viewed Internet dating as *shooting fish in a barrel,* and saw it as a sure-fire way to get laid on any given night of the week.

Take note, fellow fishermen: the fish are on to the line – "I've never done this before, but you were so..." (Most of them, anyway.) I might add that I dated all of the fish I interviewed on this subject, and find it hard (pun intended) to believe these women were truly just swept away and unable to control their behavior in that regard.

I admire the occasional fish – and they are rare – who tell the complete truth in their profile by admitting their favorite activities are watching TV and having sex. I don't actually make dates with these fish, mind you, but I admire their honesty nonetheless.

Fish of all ages will say whatever they have to say to get laid, and women of all ages – who are just as interested in getting laid as the men – feel obligated to pretend like they are virgins who have never seen a penis before, in order to ensure they will get laid, without compromising their chances of getting married too.

So consider this modification to the aforementioned rules: in short, there are no rules. Fishing is more of a game than a sport.

My advice to fish is simple: Please stop writing that your favorite thing to do is watch the sunset with a special lady while sharing a good bottle of wine. You are either gay, or you are lying, and we know it. It takes 15 minutes for the sun to set. The other 23¾ hours of the day are spent with a remote control in your wine-sipping hand, and you prefer Jack Daniels and beer to wine anyway.

Case in point: have you ever seen a boat full of real fishermen heading out for the twilight bite? I *have*, and have yet to see a bottle of wine, corkscrew, or special lady (inflatable or otherwise) loaded on to the boat. Tackle boxes, *check*; bait, *check*; beer, *check;* meat sticks, *check.* And they're off.

I would strongly suggest that women consult a book in the library, or go to the Internet, to learn all you can about the mating habits of fish before you drop a line in the pond. Almost everything you will find on fish applies to single men too. You will need a good hook: one you can hide in the soft skeleton of a worm and capture the soul of a fish when he least expects it. As he is wandering without direction from shiny lure to shiny lure, he sees yours. What you have presented for his review is as shiny as the others; offers a tasty meal for his enjoyment; but surprises him with its hard, sharp center and its perfect curve. Soon there are no shiny lures. There is daylight, there is a face, and he never knows how it happened that he was captured on that day. When he tells the story of how he was caught it will become a fish tale: the lure will be shinier and the worm will be tastier with every retelling.

Which brings me to another important aspect to fishing, which is patience. Resist the temptation to jerk your line at every nibble, and wait for a solid bite. Nibbles can feel like bites, particularly when they use phrases like - *you are the most beautiful woman I have ever seen.* You are not, and neither am I. There are many shiny lures in the pond, and it is highly unlikely that one is shinier than all others. Fish are slippery, and fish lie. It turns out fishermen tell tall tales too.

So, with these simple rules, or lack thereof, you are ready to start fishing.

Your photo is your lure; your profile your wiggly worm. Your in-box is your livewell; your response to emails is your hook. A coffee date is a bite; and a second date is when you can start to slowly turn your reel.

12

One Fish, Two Fish, Red Fish, Blue Fish

When you catch lots of fish, you can keep them on a stringer or in a livewell. With the stringer, you place a closed hook through the gill of every fish you catch and hang them on a chain from the side of the boat, dead or alive, while you keep fishing. The more humane method (and the one I prefer) is the livewell, which is a vessel of water large enough to keep a dozen or so live fish swimming around, healthy and happy, while you keep trolling. At the end of the day you decide how many fish you want for dinner and strike them on the head with a club for easy transport to the cleaning station. The young and redundant fish are released to be caught on another day.

In the real world, fishermen call this "catch and release." Sport fishermen catch and release fish without the use of a livewell. They have no interest in eating their catch, so each fish is weighed, measured and photographed before they are returned to the water without ever spending time in a livewell or on a stringer. Often fish are accidentally killed in the documentation process. For example, changing the battery in a camera, or passing the fish around to be photographed with every fisherman on the boat, may result in a fish staying out of water a little too long.

There is also the occasional fish that will swallow the hook, rather than just bite, and will be dead on arrival to the boat. These are the fish that would make me cry when I was a kid fishing with my dad. It seemed such a waste of a life that this fish was not even fit for photographs, let alone dinner, because he fell too hard for a wiggly worm.

Might I remind you that fishing is a brutal sport.

My soon-to-be-ex-husband is a sport fisherman, and I often marveled over the fact that there had never been an undocumented fish caught in his family. He, his three brothers and their father were all sport fishermen, and the walls of all of their homes contained seemingly identical photographs of men holding bloody fish - none of which died that day or kept anyone fed. I often wondered if any of these pictures were of the same fish.

We had stacks of boxes in our garage containing the documentation of fish caught by my soon-to-be-ex-grandfather-in-law, and my soon-to-be-ex-great-grandfather-in-law, may they both rest in peace. It was an impressive legacy of fish documentation.

In the winter months, my dad and I fished through holes drilled in frozen-over lakes, which probably explains my propensity to incessantly bob for the lime wedge in a vodka tonic with a splash o'cran. We never released fish back to the frozen pond, because it seemed like a rescue mission to pull live fish from an ice cube into the warmth of our little bucket. I somehow missed the correlation between our fish saving efforts and the fact that we always had fish for dinner on those nights, but I was just a minnow then.

There are many "sport fish" on the Internet, and you get to know them over time. It helps to have fishing buddies with whom to compare stories. I have four girlfriends in the pond with me – Vicki, Molly, Lisa and Linda – and we often call each other to discuss fish. Vicki or Molly will sometimes call to ask if I've heard from a fish with the username - *whateverthefish*. If I had also received an email from *whateverthefish*, we would check with the other two lines in the water, and more likely than not would all throw *whateverthefish* back.

The sport fish just nibble on every worm, wiggling or not, and usually won't even spring for a coffee date. They prefer the company of their laptop, and are probably technology geniuses living in a sequestered environment. If you manage to get one of these fish to meet you, my suggestion is to bring your club and your stringer, and strike to the head swiftly.

The conversation with every fish starts by comparing fishing stories, which can be hard at first when you don't have any, and with luck that will segue into more conversation. Sometimes it doesn't. About 20 minutes into my first date with the doctor, it became apparent the only thing we had to talk about was the fact that we were both in the pond. I threw him back.

A lawyer I dated early on had been in the pond for

a while, and had lots of good stories about disappointing first dates. I asked him – because I was assuming this was information I would soon need – how he told women he wasn't interested. He said he ended the date by saying he had a great time; that he looked forward to seeing her again; and promised to call her the next day. Then he didn't.

He turned out to be one fine fish, and I liked him. The next morning I was calling all my friends to say that my newly caught fish was a keeper, and bragging about my prowess as a fisherman. By that afternoon I remembered what he had said in the early part of our date, and that's when it hit me: the lawyer was not going to call that day like he had promised. That cunning fish had wiggled away without me even knowing he wasn't in my livewell anymore. A lesson learned.

A fish named Ron and I had a lovely night out a few months ago, and I am pretty sure I babbled on about him with the Tail Club the next day. He told me I was wonderful, which is what fish say; and that I was beautiful, which is also what fish say; and then said I was a good eater, which is not something fish usually say, which told me he was about to swim away. I never heard from Ron again, not even a polite response to my *thank you for a nice evening* note. Another lesson learned.

It seems that fish have choices too; their fate was not always in my hands. As the fisherman – the one with the tackle box, the net, the club, and the bait – I thought *I* was the one to decide who will go back in the pond and who will come home to my dinner table. Herein lies the rub: Internet fish can leave the livewell at any time.

A better way to look at Internet dating then is as if you are fishing in a Doctor Seuss book. The fish may live in a pond or a bowl, but they can fly through the air with ease, and can drive a car or a train if they need to.

Here I was thinking I was this great catch, forgetting there are many wiggly worms and shiny lures in the water competing for every tasty fish. On dry land, there are not so many choices, and it is rare for a man to just wander away from a date. Wander from a relationship, yes, but I have never been left at a Starbucks in the middle of a coffee date.

My sister Dana had inadvertently alerted me to this fact. She would tell me about this great guy she met online one day, and then his name would never come up again.

"What ever happened to Fred," I would ask.

"Fred?" she asked back. "You mean *Fish* Fred?"

She said the word "fish" like it explained everything. He was the most exciting news of the day on Wednesday, yet how could I expect her to remember *one* fish by Saturday?

It can be tricky to tell if a fish is really "on," so it's best not to try. A fisherman who keeps a hook in the water will never go hungry, so I try not to let it phase me when a fish or two jumps out of the livewell to juggle balls and drive a sports car before swan-diving back into the pond with a plate of green eggs and ham. There are plenty of fish in the pond, as the website promises, and you will release more than will escape if you're doing everything right.

13

Minnows

I am not sure who popularized the Cougar concept of dating much younger men. Was it Demi Moore? Kim Cattrell? My sister Dana? It doesn't really matter for this story, really, except I like to give credit where credit is due. The actual number of cougars outside of Hollywood or Las Vegas – in the pond or on dry land – is significantly fewer in number than most teenage boys would want to believe. Far and away the most common fish to be found in my livewell on any given day is the minnow – at least one or two tiny little fellows, needing several more years to develop into something edible – peering up at me with hopeful little smiles.

Cougars don't mind catching the little ones, but I like a little more life experience for dinner. I already have a teenage boy to eat meals with and it is hard enough to find something to talk about with Travis, besides how his grades are, and whether he brushed his teeth that day. Whatever the topic of conversation, it usually goes something like this:

"How was school today?"

"Fine."

"Did you have lunch at school or wait until you got home?"

"Chipotle."

"Did you make any new friends?"

"Whatever."

"What was your favorite class?"

"Why do you want to know?"

I hate when he starts asking questions back because my answers are seldom better than his. I already know that Phys Ed is more fun than Algebra, and I really don't care what he had for lunch that day, beyond assurance that I will not get a call from Child Protective Services because my teenager is eating from garbage cans. I just feel compelled to converse with my dinner companion and there are very few subjects a young adult male and a 50-year-old female can talk about that either will find particularly interesting.

Dinners with Travis come to mind when I get emails from minnows just a year or two older than the one I live with. Minnow emails always include the phrase "I am very mature for my age," and always point out that they "like older women." (*Duh.*)

A fish named Josh was exactly Travis' age, and he had the same poster hanging on his bedroom wall, which you could see in the background of his profile photo. Josh also looked very familiar. Upon closer inspection, it became apparent that his profile photo had been taken in Travis' bedroom, and I am pretty sure he was here for a sleepover last summer. I felt compelled to respond: "*Go to bed, it's a school night. Please have your mother call me tomorrow, and let's not tell Travis we had this conversation."*

I never heard back from Josh and I did not get a call from his mother.

I would be absolutely devastated if Travis were to take a romantic interest in one of my friends, or they in him. There's a thin line in my thinking here, but I know when the line's been crossed. If one of my friends says that Travis is becoming a handsome man, I proudly smile as if I had something to do with it. If one of them were to ask me for his cell phone number, or ask what he is doing on Friday night, I will claw their eyes out. It's that simple. My relationship with Travis is simple too: I just like knowing he is healthy and happy, somewhere close by, and that I do not need to entertain him or find him entertaining. Therefore, I imagine a date with a minnow would go something like this:

"What do you do Josh?"

"What do you mean?"

"I mean what do you do for a living?"

"I eat and I sleep and I play video games."

"Wow. That's really interesting. Do you have a favorite game?"

"Police Assault Four, I guess. Why do you want to know anyway?" Just like with Travis, my minnow would likely lose patience with my rapid-fire questioning and decide I was too annoying to spend time with.

Travis came to live with us when he was four. He is the biological son of my soon-to-be-ex-husband's youngest brother, and it was clear from the time he was born that parenting was going to be a challenge for his young parents. My brother-in-law responded to fatherhood by sinking into depression and self-medicating, and Travis' mother responded to his behavior by rebounding into a new relationship and getting pregnant again.

We started babysitting Travis a lot, and soon he became a natural extension of our family. When it came time to enroll in kindergarten, Travis' mom was between boyfriends and apartments and had three children, so we offered to take Travis full-time so he could start his education without changing schools mid-year. She was relieved, and a quickly written contract plus a few minutes with a notary was all it took to bestow us with all the rights we needed to become Travis' legal guardians.

Travis and I were very close when he was little. There was nothing I wouldn't do for the little guy, and he responded to my doting attention by being the best-behaved child who ever lived. He went to bed at exactly 9 p.m. every night without being told and woke up at 7 a.m. on the nose each day and dressed himself without drama. He would always tell me at the end of every day what his plans were for the following day, and kept to his schedule like he would be in trouble with God or Santa if he didn't.

"Tomaya I would like to have fosted fakes for bek-fast, and den to go fwimming with the wata-wings, and den I would like KFC for lunch, and den I tink we should watch Simba on tewabision, and den..." Somewhere around mid-after-noon on his itinerary review is usually when he would

fall asleep mid-sentence. Travis was a perfect little angel of a boy, and I couldn't have loved him more if I had given birth to him.

It's these tender moments from his childhood I try to remember now, because he has turned into a surly 18-year-old roommate who thinks I am just about the most frivolous human being who has ever walked the earth.

My friends often wonder why I put up with having Travis in my home. Few of them understand why I choose to live with a teenager I am not even related to, and who seems to take great pride in reminding me of how stupid and annoying I am, and in keeping the guest bathroom so dirty I would rather send people to the gas station down the street when they need use of the facilities in our fishbowl.

Travis continues to be very straightforward and literal, which is actually kind of refreshing, albeit frustrating, especially when I am trying to be profound and parental. I came home from a spa weekend once to find evidence there had been a party. Every surface had that sticky quality to it, indicating that beer and snack food were consumed in large quantities without the aid of cocktail napkins. There had been quite a few beers in the refrigerator – left over from a party I had a few weeks prior – and Travis had asked me about them, since he knows I don't like beer. I told him the beer was for guests, (since fish tend to like beer, I have found).

When I confronted Travis about his party, he responded in his usual, straightforward way: "I thought you liked to throw parties."

I stammered out a retort, realizing I had never *specifically* told Travis *he* could not have a party. So I switched gears and said it was not right for he and his underage friends to drink alcohol, and that it was especially not okay for them to drink MY alcohol.

"But you said the beer was for guests," he said, "and I had guests." He had me.

This black and white kid could trump my shades-of-grey reasoning without fail every time. Unencumbered by middle age and responsibility, Travis is simply smarter than me.

One thing that I do have over other parents of surly teenagers is this: I got to experience what life would be like if Travis were not in my life, and I can still bring all of the emotion of it back at will when I need to.

I had just completed the last day of a wilderness experience – where my classmates and I were completely sequestered from cell phones and laptops for seven days – as part of my American Leadership Forum fellowship training. I was feeling about as spiritually centered as I had ever been when one of the ALF staffers took me aside. "I have a phone message for you," she said with a look of grave concern on her face. My knees buckled on the word "message," because I had given strict instructions to everyone at home and at work that the emergency phone number was to be used for life and death situations only.

So I was already on my knees when she delivered the first blow.

"Travis is dead." *Blow number one.*

"He committed suicide this morning." *Blow number two, and I was down.*

I realized at that moment I was not as strong a person as I thought I was, because this news was simply impossible to absorb. My body collapsed, as if my skeleton had disintegrated into grains of sand. All my voice could do was make guttural sounds, and I think I was just saying, "can't... can't... can't..." as if my soul was rejecting this information with every fiber of its being.

It took about 30 minutes for me to gain the composure I needed to use the only landline on the island to phone home. When I did, I learned that the message – which had originated from my office to the ALF office; from the ALF office to the ranger station, where it was answered by the teenage son; from the teenage son, to the ranger, to the only landline on the island and then to the ALF wilderness staffer; and finally to me – was supposed to be: "Travis' DAD is dead. He committed suicide this morning." Only one word had been dropped from the original message in this game of *Telephone*, but it was a vital word.

I was very sad to learn my brother-in-law had lost his life-long battle with Bi-polar Disorder, but you would not have known by the rapidity of which my skeleton reconstituted and from the smile on my face. I had been given a second chance with Travis, which every parent or guardian should have the opportunity to experience. That half-hour of thinking he was gone – and the sense of failure that engulfed me upon learning he had taken his own young life – took me to dark places where humor cannot thrive. Emerging from that place, and knowing I could still make sure

Travis was the happiest boy on the planet, was life affirming. A gift. It was as if this rebirth of Travis made me his real mother after all.

So it would come to be that as long as Travis continues to take breath he will be free to drink the beer meant for fish and to keep his bathroom as filthy as he sees fit. Just let me hear the moldy showerhead come on every morning so I will know he still sweats when he sleeps; which means his body is still warm, his heart is still beating, and blood still circulates through his veins; and I can get through anything life throws at me knowing my baby boy will live to see another day.

I really dread the day when Travis moves out and leaves me really alone for the first time in my life. Still, I have a hard time coming up with things we can do together, besides maybe eat, and I will always have trouble finding things to talk about when we eat together. Which brings me back to the cougar/minnow phenomenon, and my refusal to play in that tournament.

Besides my sister Dana, the only cougar I know is my workout partner Vanessa, a beautiful former model who never had children of her own. That lack of a reference frame is probably what allowed her to maintain a two-year relationship with a 22 year-old when she was in her late 40s. She said she was always telling him what to wear and what to say, but soon found herself also telling him how to hold his fork, and then making him eat his vegetables. One day it dawned on her that she was in more of a guardianship than a relationship, and they broke up. Several years later Vanessa met and married an age appropriate Silicon Valley executive, but still feels compelled to prance around in animal prints occasionally, just to remind mothers everywhere of what she is capable of.

I feel fortunate to actually be attracted to men my own age, and feel a little sorry for the men and women who are not. Sometimes I am not so nice on that subject, as there's nothing I hate more than the sight of a grey-haired man with a young girl in her twenties who are clearly not a doting dad and his daughter. (My dad and I are still close, and still do things together – like go skiing – and I always find it disturbing when people sometimes mistake us for a couple.)

A young, college-age girl who lives on an upper floor of my building was often in the company of an older man I recognized to be the CEO of a multinational technology company. He is somewhat of a celebrity to people who read the business section of the newspaper, but even in Silicon Valley he probably walks the streets in relative obscurity. I wrongly assumed the CEO was my neighbor's father. When I learned from the doorman that the girl was really his mistress, I actually went home and threw up. Luckily, I never saw them together again, because I would have had difficulty refraining from scolding him and psychoanalyzing her, and it takes several days to get the smell of vomit out of an elevator.

Mike was giddy to report that a beautiful twenty-something girl from our health club had asked him out one day. It was as if he had just been granted permission from God to do something his better instinct would not have initiated on its own accord. When he told me her age – which was right between the ages of my two stepsons, and 20 years his junior – my mind went to Nate at three and Ben at seven, and to a time I carried one on my shoulders and one in my arms home from a Sharks hockey game, to which little Ben noted made me "very strong for a mom." The mother's instinct is in me, and it was Travis, Ben and Nate's very strong mom that hauled off and punched my friend Mike on the arm as hard as I could to his bewildered astonishment.

Mike uncharacteristically wore long sleeves to work for the next few days and he never mentioned the minnow girl from the club again, although I am pretty sure he still saw her after that.

14
Charming Fish

My sisters found joy in girlish activities like sewing clothes for Barbie dolls and helping mom bake cookies when we were kids. I always found what dad was doing on any given Saturday to be more interesting. Take apart the car? *What fun!* Drill a hole in the ice and catch the fish trapped inside? *Count me in!*

As cute as my parents thought it was to have three girls and one rambunctious pseudo-boy, by the time I reached puberty – and my mother had still never seen me in a dress – she enrolled me in Charm School to reclaim the daughter she gave birth to. Thanks to this special "lady" training, I soon learned how to properly fit a bra (although I was several years from needing one) and mastered the art of walking with a book on my head. Book balancing seemed like an athletic feat so I embraced it wholeheartedly, and took great joy at being able to walk around my house and even up stairs with the Webster's Dictionary propped on my crown, although I occasionally used my training bra as a book support by wrapping it around the book and fastening it under my chin.

Book running became a competitive sport in our house, and I soon championed sprinting the length of our backyard faster than all my siblings while balancing a book, which was not much competition considering my older sister had grown sizeable breasts by then that slowed her down, and my younger sisters had stubby little toddler legs. (My personal trainer today blames my swayback tendencies, and subsequent lower back problems, on all the book walking/running I did as a child.)

Mastering this new sport did not please my mother, so I was drafted into year two of Charm School. I defiantly attended each session with arms crossed at my still flat chest and refused to take part in the taming of me. We were moving from Minneapolis to San Jose that year because my dad had gotten an engineering job in the computer sciences field. I didn't know what a computer was back then, but my dad explained that he was going to design machines like the robot on *Lost in Space*. I was pretty sure they wouldn't have something like Charm School in the hippest, happiest place on earth; where Mickey Mouse, movie stars and robots roamed the snow-free streets freely, or so I imagined, but I was wrong.

Within months of settling in to our new home in San Jose, my mother found the *Sally Sears School for Young Charmers* and I was enrolled. It became clear to me then that I was going to be the oldest pupil in the history of the Sears Charm School if I didn't master this acting-like-a-lady bit fast. I made it my mission to convince "Sally" and my mother that I was the most charming, ladylike and sophisticated 11 year old the world had ever seen. I did this without giving up my second life as dad's fishing buddy, but I reconciled the duality by putting worms on a hook with my pinky extended, and sorting the lures in my tackle box both by color and by their appropriateness for evening or daytime wear. A transformation was beginning to take place. Or so they thought.

The truth is I faked my way through the final year of Charm School in order to appease my mother, and faked it so well that I was crowned "Sally's Perfect Charmer" at the Fashion Show/Graduation event. I won that honor by writing an essay titled "Fashion Sense Makes Common Sense," which dripped with flowery prose and sage advice on choosing clothes and accessories. I clearly didn't have the capitalist instinct yet, or I would have sold my award-sure essay a dozen times over to one lucky little girl at hundreds of Sears stores throughout the country where this ritual was taking place in store basements chain-wide.

The memory is surreal: a long stroll down the runway with a bouquet of roses held in the crook of my arm, as "Sally" read excerpts from my fashion essay over the loudspeaker to the accompaniment of Tom Jones singing *She's a Lady*. What I remember most was seeing the tears of joy in my mother's eyes, the look of sheer disbelief on my father's face, and hearing the sound of polite clapping. My grandmother was there too, I recall, and was in the advanced stages of dementia by then. Until the day she died 15 years later she remained convinced that one of her granddaughters was Miss America, but could never remember which of the six held the title.

When I think back at the values Sears Roebuck and Company tried to instill in us, I can't help but marvel that this was the summer of 1969, and a sexual revolution was being waged just 40 miles away in San Francisco, and San Jose's only head-shop had opened directly across the street from the Meridian Avenue Sears store in which (or *under* which in this case) I received my formal training on basic girl-dom. I was witnessing the end of an era wherein women were trained for subservience and good nature, and look back at it now with the kind of self-awe people must feel when they were on the scene for an important historical event.

So what does all this charm school talk have to do with fishing the Internet for dates? Absolutely nothing, and that's my point. If you attended *Sally Sears School for Young Charmers* – or a like institution wherein you were taught how to behave at a dance, or what to say to a boy who has asked you on a date – then it is crucially important for you to reprogram the way you think before dropping a line in the pond. On this point I cannot be more clear: IF YOU OBEY THE RULES LEARNED IN CHARM SCHOOL, YOU WILL BE SINGLE FOR THE REST OF YOUR LIFE.

I came across my Charm School notes recently when I happened upon a box of memorabilia from my childhood. In my adolescent handwriting, I read with shock notebooks brimming with bad advice about how to behave in social situations, and how to remain chaste in the dating world. Here are a few excerpts, along with my present-day notations of the wrongness of each statement:

"Never ask a boy on a date, and only telephone a boy if you are returning his call." [Single women over 50 are aggressive. Waiting for the telephone to ring means you're not in the game.]

"Dance with every boy who asks you. It's never polite to hurt someone's feelings." ["I'm not drunk enough to dance yet" is a better response, because it will preserve his feelings and guarantee you receive a complimentary beverage.]

"Do not giggle when you are looking at a boy you like. He will think you are laughing at him." [Of course you are laughing at him. Most men (especially Caucasians) look ridiculous when they dance!]

"Find one good girlfriend to sit with at a dance, and refrain from talking to each other too much. Boys will not approach a gaggle of girls, and will recoil from girls they believe are partaking in foolish gossip." [Here's a better idea - find one girlfriend to make-out with at the dance. Men cannot resist a little girl-on-girl action.]

"Do not stand and dance at the sidelines of the dance floor, as it will appear you are too eager and "easy." Instead, sit with your legs to one side (not crossed) and your hands placed on one knee, and contain your appreciation of the music to the slight movement of your head." [If you like the song, go out on the dance floor by yourself and just dance. You don't need a man drooling down your lucky blouse to enjoy yourself.]

"It's never okay to slap a boy in public, no matter what he has said or done. Find a nearby gentleman to report the incident to, and let them handle it man-to-man. [I prefer a knee to the groin, but I can't imagine what a man could say or do to me at 50 years old that I would find shocking and offensive today. (Although my husband's girlfriend calling in the middle of his "you're great but I'm leaving" speech *was* a little offensive.)]

And my personal favorite for completely eliminating a woman's right to choose:

"When a boy asks you for a date, your answer is "yes." You can politely decline a second date, but every boy should be given the opportunity to impress you." [Clearly written before the Internet. On-line, the profile is their opportunity to impress you. No need to have coffee with someone who didn't.]

If I were to open a Charm School today, the advice I would give to young women would be very different from the lessons I learned. I would teach girls how to make a decent martini, because men love to see a woman at work on a martini shaker. I would tell them the only thing more painful than childbirth is a tattoo removal procedure, and I would teach them how to mask teeth marks with an hourly dusting of tinted mineral powder. I would teach them to respect their elders, but also to envy them; because 30 isn't old, 40 is about when you reach true adulthood, and 50 is when life gets fun.

15

Married Men Can't Swim

I know what "F" stands for. It's "fuck-buddy," right?

That's what I get for letting a man use my cell phone – a happily married business associate who could not resist the temptation to peruse my contact list while he had the opportunity. I guess it's the modern day equivalent to a bachelor in the swinging '60s handing his little black book over to his secretary for just a moment. Of course she's going to open it and browse through names.

The letter "F" is how I designate fish on my cell phone. Scattered throughout a contact list of friends, family and business associates are a fairly lengthy number of common man names followed by an "F." John-F, Bob3-F, Mike-F, Gary-F... and so on.

I believe it's important to put fish in your cell phone as soon as numbers are exchanged. Without the prompter, it can be embarrassing to get a call from someone who says, "Hi, it's the guy you were chatting with on *Plenty of Fish*," and still have no idea who's calling. Worst yet, a fish you have already dated calls with the kind of familiarity reserved for close friends and lovers. It seems to make them happy when you know their name, even if they are just one of many fish.

Married men, particularly the devout monogamists, are fascinated with the sex lives of single women. They believe we are either starved for male company or that we maintain an unlimited supply of "boy toys" to service our wanton desires.

"I'll bet you're a cougar," said the husband of one of my girlfriends at a party one night. "If I were a woman, I would be a cougar," he continued.

Not that I had to ask, but I did anyway: "Why?"

"Because the young guys just want to screw all the time, and they like doing it with older women, and I would think you'd want to take advantage of that."

I explained that the concept of sleeping with someone I could have given birth to was repulsive to me, and he seemed disappointed at that. Quick to recover his fantasy, he assured me I would have no trouble getting laid, even if I did have very high standards for a single woman of 50.

This is perhaps the only change for the worst since I have been single. Happily married men treat me differently than they did before. They are not as friendly; never comment on my appearance, like they used to; and go out of their way to avoid being alone with me. I guess it's okay to flirt with a married woman if you're a married man, without upsetting anyone. Another guy's wife is fair game, and all in good fun. Most importantly, married women are safe. Single women, on the other hand, are viewed as temptresses. They fear we will try to break up their marriage in retaliation for the fact that someone interfered with our matrimonial bliss. I am only speculating as to their reasoning, of course, but it's something I deal with on a fairly regular basis because the vast majority of men I know are married; and most are married to women I like very much.

I am referring now to the typical behavior of a monogamous male. These men are completely harmless in every way, since they have learned to contain their vicarious nature to simply flirting with the wives of their friends and the friends of their wives. They deny their basic instinct by staying clear of single women, particularly the recently divorced.

The more typical male – which, statistically speaking, is married – is considerably more discrete, and usually limits his extra-curricular activities to business trips and boys' weekends. I know this only because I have always been more popular when I travel. Russ from Philadelphia... Phil from Fort Worth... Steve from Cincinatti... the orthopedic surgeon from Oregon... the pharmaceutical salesman from Connecticut... the retired hockey player from Colorado... the list goes on and on. I did not actually have sex with any of these men, but each told me the sad story of the wife who didn't understand him, and each made himself available to me. "One night only," they said, like they were offering themselves up for a limited time and at a very special price. These married men are always surprised when I don't jump on the opportunity (no pun intended.)

On the road, married men are straightforward

about their status, but closer to home I have found wayward husbands to be masters at manipulating the English language. The term "separated," it seems, means different things to different people. To me and almost everyone I know, it is a legal distinction single people make between a person who is divorced – meaning the paperwork has been stamped and officially decreed by the State of California – versus someone, like me, who is out of their marriage but not yet legal. These are people, like me, who don't have the time or the money, and aren't fighting over anything so making it legal isn't a priority. We're emotionally and financially separated from our spouses, but we don't have the paperwork to prove it. It's kind of like living together before marriage in reverse.

It seems that many married men I encounter believe themselves to be "separated" any time they are in public without their wives. While it may be true linguistically, the truly monogamous do not consider themselves "separated" every time they leave for work in the morning. I dated a few married-but-temporarily-separated men inadvertently in the early days, until Kathy told me about the cheater's code one night at a Tail Club meeting. She said the litmus test was where they lived, and whether you were free to visit them at their house. It's also a good bet they're still married if they claim to live in a house, since apartments and condos are usually where you find the recently separated. I lost a few fish to that litmus test, and it surprised me how quickly they came clean when I asked to pick them up at their house. They weren't liars, after all, because they had truly convinced themselves that their game of semantics was fair and accurate.

Hotel bars and golf resorts is where I have gathered most of my data on married men, and I believe I have enough data to surmise that there is a whole lot of adultery going on out there. So I was not completely surprised to learn there is actually a dating site for married people on the Internet. *Ashley Madison* advertises mostly on sports programs and male-dominated radio stations with the slogan – *Life is short. Have an affair.* Their logo is a key.

The name *Ashley Madison* comes from the two most popular baby names for girls, "Ashley" and "Madison." The genesis of the website name has a high creep rating to me, considering many of the married men using this site probably have little girls at home with one of those names. What does this say about the typical married man, I wonder? My natural curiosity drove me to learn more.

Unlike more traditional dating sites, there are seldom photos on *Ashley Madison*, so you cannot rely on the science of physiognomy to make your selections. The profiles include less information about values and principles, and more about sexual desires and preferences. There is also a great deal of information about availability. Some of the men say they are only available for mid-day encounters, while others say they can get away any time for the right opportunity. I know all of this because the sociologist in me just couldn't resist becoming a member. I listed myself as a "single woman looking for married encounters," and then sat back to read the email pitches that poured in.

The iconic element to *Ashley Madison* is a key. Once I had chatted with someone for a while and determined he was not someone I knew, we would exchange keys. Only with a key can you check out the on-line portfolio of a one-night-stand candidate. The portfolio includes photos of your prospective sex partner, and is significantly less civilized than *Plenty of Fish* or *Match.com*. I was allowed access to graphic pictures of body parts on a few occasions where I was warranted worthy of a key. *"Here's my nine-inch penis." "Here's a close-up of my six-pack abs." "Here's my butt, taken over my shoulder in the bathroom mirror,"* (where I can't help but notice upon review of the vanity accoutrement that his wife uses the same Clinique body spray as I do.)

While *Plenty of Fish* will disallow graphic photos and nudity of any kind, *Ashley Madison* allows it, but warns you right after you insert your key that you are about to view graphic content. Seems a fitting policy for a website named after two little girls.

Ashley Madison is interesting to me not just as an amateur sociologist and a female, but also as an advertising professional. How does this so-called "dating site" manage to have almost as many registered women as men when it only makes itself known to men? It doesn't take a degree in marketing to know that buying airtime on heavy metal radio stations and sporting events is not going to get you a lot of registered female users. And yet this site exists, and connections are made.

I wanted to demonize these men as cheaters of the worst kind. These were not innocents who found themselves tempted away from monogamy by a "hottie" at the office, or a recently divorced neighbor. These men are not driven astray; they are premeditating their infidelity. If there were levels of adultery, I would think this to be the first degree. A sociologist is always looking to understand human behavior, so I started chatting with a few of these demons to see if I could figure out what made them tick.

I didn't respond to the men who sent me pictures of body parts, but I did talk to two men I met on *Ashley Madison*, and was surprised to find they were nice guys. Vince was a man who had not had sex for five years, but was extremely committed to keeping his family together. In his mind, having a discrete affair with a willing partner – preferably one in the same circumstance – was his only chance to have his physical needs met, while remaining true to his family-guy principles. Ray knew his wife was having an affair with her boss, and it was pretty much common knowledge to everyone in their circle. He wanted to retaliate, for his own peace of mind, but did not want to publicly humiliate her or cause further embarrassment to their teenage children.

Vince and Ray were decent guys who were trying to do the right thing in their own strange way, and I found myself oddly moved by their respective stories. I registered on this degenerate website to conduct research on sleazy, slimy, cheating men who oozed insincerity and dishonesty from every pore. To say I was disappointed would be an understatement.

My short time on *Ashley Madison* was great for my self-esteem. I received 50 or 60 emails to every one I get on *Plenty of Fish*, and a not-surprising number of the emails I received started with *"Wow. I think you are a real woman."* The men I actually chatted with seemed pretty normal by societal standards, excepting their dues-paid membership in *Ashley Madison*. It was a catalytic experience nonetheless. I am not sure I will ever be able to look at a man who is uttering the words "until death do us part" again without thinking of the picture of "Stan's" penis or "Jerry's" wife's Clinique products in the picture behind her husband's naked white ass.

16
Size Matters

Everyone exaggerates in his or her on-line profiles. Generally, women subtract a few years from their age, and men add a few inches to their height. And both sexes lie about their physique, but it's hard not to. *Plenty of Fish* provides only six multiple-choice descriptions of body type from which to choose, and you can only select one. "Morbidly obese" is not a choice, so a 400-pounder can only claim to be carrying "a few extra pounds." I learned that if I was meeting someone for coffee who said he is "average," to prepare myself to meet a man who was overweight. If a man said he was "athletic," he would probably just be what I would call "average," but not always.

The highest-ranking physical description provided on *Plenty of Fish* is "athletic," so I was taken aback on a couple coffee dates when I found myself seated across from a fish the size of Arnold Schwarzenegger in his Mr. Universe days. The six choices do not include "muscle-bound," or "steroid-enhanced physique," so I guess they cannot be accused of lying. The physical descriptors are the same for men and women, so if you have

Pamela Anderson's body, you could only describe yourself as "thin" or "athletic." I guess you could choose "a few extra pounds" and then make note in the profile that the extra pounds are all in two places.

As for height, men under 5' 10" tall will add two inches. Therefore, if they said they were 5' 10", they were 5' 8". If they said they were 5' 8", they were actually 5' 6". I had one coffee date with a man who claimed to be 5' 10" tall. When we stood face-to-face it was immediately apparent that we were about the same height, so he went on the offense. The first words out of his mouth (before "hello, you must be...") were, "you lied about your height; because there is no way you are only 5' 5". I admired his chutzpah, but threw him back in the pond anyway.

My first husband was 5' 8", the second and third were both 5' 10", so it was not-to-type that my first five dates were well over six feet tall. 6'2", 6'2", 6"3", and then there was Rick at 6'5" and weighing in at 248 pounds, none of which was body fat. He was my biggest catch.

At some point in my fishing I stopped looking at height as a variable, and always expected my coffee dates to be very tall men. Therefore, when I went to meet a fish named Craig for coffee I was expecting to be towered over, and found myself disappointed to find he was only 5'8". The next day I described him to friends as a "puny little thing."

What was wrong with me? Craig was nice and he was cute, and he had not an ounce of body fat on him, but I couldn't reconcile his diminutive size. In a relatively short period of time, I had become a height snob. Poor Craig just made the mistake of being my first coffee date with a man under 6' 2".

Rick, my biggest fish, was fine in every way until he told me about his multiple arrests for assault. This surprised me, because he seemed the gentle giant, and was probably the smartest fish I had the privilege to meet. How could this intelligent, seemingly kind man be prone to violence? It just didn't seem possible.

By our third date he finally felt comfortable enough to tell me some of the stories, and I learned that Rick was a big guy with an even bigger temper. I laughed about it at the time, because it seemed so unlikely this wonderful man could do harm to anyone. The next day I thought about it more, and my mind wandered to the many, many ways in which I have made the men in my life angry over the years, and concluded that Big Rick was not someone I would ever want to make angry. Could I sustain a relationship with a man without ever making him angry? Probably not, but I thought I could maintain a benign state of calm for a few more dates at least.

On our fourth date I learned that Rick and I shared a dangerous passion for speed. We were driving to a restaurant a few miles away using back roads, because something about his Porsche was not street legal. It had four tires, two seats and a steering wheel, so I had no reason to believe it a vehicle not capable of getting us to a restaurant in Palo Alto, and had no misgivings when he issued the warning.

We were only on the road for a minute or so when

he looked at me with a bad-boy smile and said, "Ready?" I said I was, and he hit the accelerator. We were at 100 mph in seconds, and the speedometer was still climbing. We got to 175 before he had to downshift to turn a corner. We took the corner at about 105, and two wheels were off the ground. It was exhilarating, and I wanted nothing more than to do it again. So we did it again, and we did it again.

I don't remember if it was Kathy or Linda or Molly who said it first when I reported the date details to the Tail Club, but the general consensus was this: Rick was going to kill me. No one thought he would murder me in a premeditated, psychopathic kind of way, but they saw how he brought out aspects of my personality best kept deeply buried in my adolescence, and they didn't see how this could end well.

When I was a teenager, there were a couple of roads near my house where I would take my car late at night when no one was around, and see how fast I could make it go. I loved the rush of seeing the red line on the speedometer go higher and higher, and believe the tires left the road a couple times when I got to somewhere around 120 mph. That was my guilty pleasure and no one - not even my closest friends, and certainly not my parents - knew about my 3 a.m. drag races at the time. I never got caught, and I never crashed, but I shared my teenage racing stories with the Tail Club years later.

The dreams I had when I was going through my speed demon phase always ended in a crash. The "ball of fire" dream, as I came to know it, was recurring and always ended with me in a car rolling over and over again in a ball of flames. I would always wake up right before the car came to a final stop – before they pulled my mangled corpse out of the charred wreckage.

I started having that dream again some time after the fifth date with Rick.

As always, the Tail Club girls were right. Continuing to date a speed demon twice my size would most likely result in my untimely demise. Of that I was certain. He would either kill me with his bare hands when I pushed the wrong button, which I will inevitably do some day; or we would die together in a spectacular, high-speed car crash. I reluctantly released him.

After sending Rick back to the pond I started to wonder if I was acting too much like Goldilocks. There are too many choices, and the sheer number of choices has perhaps made me too picky. Every one of the men I met on-line would have been very interesting to me if I had met them anywhere on dry land. But because they are pulled from a sea of fish, they are put under extreme, close scrutiny, which often results in their release. Was there such a thing as "just right?"

Not too big, not too small.

Not too hot, not too cold.

Athletic, but not muscle-bound.

Tall, but not scary.

Not fat, but not puny.

Fast, but not a speed demon with a death wish.

Like me, but not too much like me…

Or perhaps I am finally honing in on what I am looking for.

17
When Fish Dump

The most pronounced difference between men and women, in my opinion, is how they respond to and/or initiate a break-up. With men, it's simply over when it's over and there's no point in expressing angst about it. When Mike's relationship ended with a woman he had been seeing for more than a year, he didn't even mention it to me – the business partner and friend who starts every day with the same question: "How are you?"

Months after the split (apparently) he stated calmly that it was over when I suggested the two of them might enjoy a romantic restaurant I had just discovered.

"Thanks," he said. "Good to know for future reference, but I'm not feeling romantic about anyone in particular right now." And that was all he felt like sharing.

Women need to be surrounded by friends after a break-up, and I've comforted many a girlfriend through days, weeks, months, and sometimes years of post-breakup analysis about what went wrong or who was at fault: a discussion that often takes a dark and inward turn to the recently-dumped woman wondering if she will ever find anyone who could tolerate her many, many faults. It is at this point in the process where a girlfriend's role is to prop up the injured party with praise and admiration, while pointing out the many obvious faults and weaknesses of the newly departed fish. "You're too good for him." "You're so pretty he must have been intimidated." "If Fat Faye can meet someone and get married at 56, then surely you, with all your wonderful qualities, can find someone too." Some of the calming statements are canned; others are customized for the victim.

Of all my single friends, Molly is perhaps most needy in this regard; emotionally needy, that is. Molly is arguably the most financially secure single member of the Tail Club, as she still profits from her ex-husband's lucrative patents and is ridiculously well paid for babysitting a prima-dona CEO. She fishes in a richer pond than the rest of us; a site called Millionaire-dot-com, which requires submission of a notarized net worth statement to become a certified member of this exclusive fishing club. Molly is also less starved for male attention than the rest of us, most of whom live alone. She spends her days at the side of her handsome employer, and her nights at home with her young adult son and the houseboy who keeps her palatial residence operational for free room and board plus a small salary. For this I am the most envious of Molly. She actually employs a man to do man-stuff at her house – the one challenge even highly independent single women like Vicki struggle with on an almost daily basis.

When Molly gets dumped – which is what we call it, even if the break-up is mutual or initiated by the girlfriend – there is not enough vodka in the world or girlfriends in the Tail Club to calm her down. As much as we try to talk her out of it, she is one of those women who can't stop herself from calling or emailing the man to beg him back after she's had a few drinks, and we've propped her up with compliments. The confidence she gains from her girlfriends makes her question how said man could not love her, and her pleading emails result in her getting dumped all over again. The healing process has to begin anew, and is repeated again and again with Molly.

Rejection is rejection, and I imagine it's hard on a man too. I think the real difference between men and women in this regard then is that women are just better at ending relationships, and can release a fish with his ego and confidence intact. Nurturing the fragile male ego is something we all learn in charm school. Men tend to prefer the quick and honest approach – likening it to pulling off an adhesive bandage – and often choose a perfunctory text or email over a face-to-face encounter to break the news.

"I met someone else. Sorry," was the text Molly received one day from her boyfriend of six months. When she suggested a face-to-face closure discussion that weekend, his brutally honest reply was "Can't do. I'm helping my girlfriend move in to my house this weekend." Poor Molly. Rejection by replacement is most definitely the worst kind of break-up, because it's hard not to take personally the news that someone else has been deemed the better catch.

When my husband told me he was moving out it was a businesslike face-to-face meeting at the office, so I already had my fingers on the keyboard when he got past "it's been a good 20 years... I have no regrets... you're a great person... yadda, yadda, BUT..." On the word "but" I hit *send* on the SOS email I had been composing to the Tail Club, which said simply, "He's OUT. Meet at The Grill NOW!"

When Bob3 broke up with me, he did so with a bouquet of roses and a box of candy on Valentine's Day. The email I got right after they were delivered gushed on about what a wonderful person I was and how much I deserved to be recognized with gifts on Valentine's Day. Then it said he felt our relationship had run its course and he wouldn't be calling me again. It seems the candy and flowers were lovely parting gifts.

Mike2 dumped me in an email too. We had made loose plans early in the week to go out on Friday night. When Friday came around, and I still hadn't heard from Mike2, I started to wonder whether I had a date that night or not. Mid-day, I nudged him by email to see if he still wanted to see me or if I should make other plans. Two hours later he replied:

You say things that rub me the wrong way a lot. You compare me to other men, which I hate, and you accuse me of lying when I say I have other plans. If you can be adult enough to have a rational conversation, then feel free to call.

If not, have a nice life. - M

It was apparent we were NOT going to have a date that night, and I sure as hell did not feel like being an adult about it. I was devastated. Not because I was gaga for Mike2, since I wasn't feeling "it" with him after our two dates. His assertion that I was an offensive, man-comparing, slanderous, non-adult left me dazed and confused, on top of the usual feeling of rejection. I desperately needed to consume vodka, and lots of it; surrounded by girlfriends, and lots of them, as soon as possible.

Fortunately, I had enough Tail Clubbers respond to my S.O.S. text – "Dumped. The Grill NOW" – that I got my wish soon enough. By about 6 p.m., I was in the process of ordering my third vodka/diet tonic with a splash o' cran when my cell phone started to ring. It was Mike2 (in my cell phone as Mike2-F.) I sent him to voicemail and continued to drink. Soon my phone started flashing red lights and vibrating, which either meant I had text messages coming in or that my table was ready. I wasn't waiting for a table, so the cell phone was dropped in my purse so that pesky Mike2 couldn't distract me from the task of drinking to forget him.

By eight o'clock I had consumed enough vodka and was thoroughly propped up with enough girlfriend love to pull a "Molly" and call Mike2. The conversation did NOT go as I expected.

"I am ruddeee to have an adult con-vers-say-shun wit chew now."

"Excuse me? Are you drunk?"

"Yesss, I am drunk. This is what I do when I get dumped."

"Dumped? Who dumped you?"

"You did."

"No, I didn't"

"Yes you did. I got an email."

"Oh my God. I just figured out what happened. I sent that email to the wrong girl! Oh baby, I would not have dumped YOU, you are one of my favorites!"

"But you spelled my name right."

"The other woman has the same name as you, and spells it the same unusual way."

"Really?"

"Well, why would I dump you and then call to confirm our date? Can you think of any logical reason why anyone would do that?"

"No," I said realizing that I had never listened to his voicemail messages. His logic was starting to make sense to me in my inebriated state.

"Okay then. It's still early. Let me come downtown right now and take you out to dinner."

"Sure. I mean, no. I mean, we're okay, I guess, but downtown is spinning too much to land your car here. I think I will just go home and throw up now."

The next morning I woke up with a slight hangover, and remembered Mike2 referring to me as "one of" his favorites. Should this upset me? (I, too, am seeing other fish, after all.) I decided to let it go and see how and when Mike2 would make it up to me. The flowers would probably arrive by noon; a gushing apology delivered by email; or maybe he would just show up in person, on his knees, begging my forgiveness. We shall see.

It was Sunday afternoon before I finally got the call I was expecting from Mike2.

He was already yelling at me when I said "Hello."

"Why won't you get it through your head that I did not break up with you? All these mean and crazy emails you are sending me are just wrong, and I don't deserve to be treated this way for making a simple mistake! You have a common name, for God's sake."

"Uh, Mike? I didn't send you any emails today or yesterday."

"What? Well who did then?"

"Maybe it was the woman with the same name as me who you dumped by email on Friday?"

"You could be right. That makes sense."

"Yes. Women can get kind of hysterical when they get dumped. I would know, because I just got dumped myself, and I was pretty upset there for a while..."

"You did not get dumped."

"Yes I did."

"No you didn't."

"Yes I did. For two or three hours on Friday I lived the *I just got dumped* heartache, so don't take that away from me."

"I can and I will take it away from you because for the last time... YOU were not dumped!" (This is sounding less and less like the adult conversation I had envisioned.)

"OK, fine. Explain it to me again now that I am sober."

"Well, I have you in my phone and in my email by a different name, so I wouldn't confuse you with the other girls *(note plural)* with the same name. So whenever you send me a message and sign your real name, it just throws me off, because I think you're this crazy girl by the same name who is stalking me."

"So I should use a different name?"

"Well, yes, that would make things easier."

The idea of changing my name to continue having ridiculous conversations with Mike2 seemed like a really bad idea to me, but I told him I would give it some thought.

Later in the day, I did a little fishing and made a coffee date with another Mike. As I entered his name in my cell phone (Mike3-F), I realized I had never gotten any of my Mikes or my Bobs mixed up, and I wasn't asking any of them to change their names, and I started wondering how many of the conversations I had with Mike2 were *my* conversations, and how many of them were meant for someone else. It would explain what I had described to my friends as his "moodiness," in he would sometimes sound really happy to hear from me on the phone, and other times it would seem as if I was bothering him.

That was it. I decided at that moment I was done with Mike2. Now it was my turn to write an email.

Mike –

I have decided to take your advice and change my name so you will be absolutely sure who it is that dumped you. Enjoy the rest of your life without me, and happy fishing!

- Holly G.

18

Mikes, Bikes and Hikes

While my first three Internet dates were with men named Bob, Bob did not turn out to be the most prolific name for fish who bit on my hook. My numerical system was put to the test by the preponderance of Mikes in my livewell, and eventually having that name alone was enough to merit immediate release. Which is too bad because despite a string of bad dates with fish by that name I like the name Mike. It rhymes with lots of happy words, (i.e. like, bike, tike, hike) which is really handy when you're writing poetry. I think I have only met one man named Mike who I thought was truly evil – in 50 years and hundreds of Mikes – so that's saying quite a bit.

There was a time when there were so many Mikes at the agency we had to give them all monikers: *Michael, Mikey, Big Mike* and *Original Mike*. And then there was *401K Mike, Wendy's Mike* and *Client Mike*, and my personal trainer is named Mike (*Trainer Mike*) to add to the confusion.

So after Mike4 (which is technically my fifth Mike when you factor in the friend and business partner by that name without an assigned number) I had to start releasing perfectly fine fish because they had the wrong name. I realize this makes me far more like Goldilocks and far less like Holly Golightly, but I did not want to become like Mike2 and get my fish mixed up, and I know my limitations when it comes to numerals.

My fellow fishermen could relate to my Mike problem. Vicki was getting a lot of Joes; Molly was in Tom-land; Linda was a mark for Marks; and Lisa seemed to only attract men with uncommon names. My sister Dana had a *Funny Kevin* and a *Tall Kevin* she was dating at the same time, but I haven't asked her if that was a pattern or a fluke. Is there a cosmic force at play, I wonder? Do we attract men with certain names if we have a special liking of that name? Or do we like the name because fish who bear the name seem to like us? Just something to think about (as if I didn't have enough to think about.)

Something we have all found to be true is that men over 50 of every name have motorcycles (Harleys mostly) and they ALL include photos of their two-wheeled, big boy toy on their profile page. The motorcycle shot is as standard and as expected as a photo of the good-looking kids, if such creatures exist. "But my Harley is very rare," said one of my fish dates after showing me a picture of his Heritage Nostalgia Softtail Harley Davidson that looked exactly like the *very rare* Heritage Nostalgia Softtail Harley I had *rode bitch on* just three days before.

"Why are men so predictable?" asked Molly one

night after her third date with a weekend road warrior. "There is no female equivalent. What do women buy at mid-life to prove we are still a force to be reckoned with?"

"Botox," said Vicki. "We inject ourselves with toxins to freeze our facial muscles so we can have a subtly less wrinkled forehead" she added, which changed the conversation from one of "aren't men ridiculous" to another one about the extreme measures we will take to preserve just a little of our fading beauty.

Vicki was a little on edge that night because she had just agreed to rendezvous with a fish at a nearby park for a three-mile hike in a very remote location. She set the date for two weeks out so she could make the hike on her own and test her ability on the trail. I agreed to accompany her on a practice hike the next weekend.

I surmised that this must be a very special fish for Vicki to go to such an effort to make an impression, but she preferred to think of the hike as embarking on a new weekend activity. Vicki had recently experienced three disappointing coffee dates in a week, so her pessimism about meeting the man of her dreams on the Internet was increasing.

"People our age go on hikes," she explained, pointing out that "hiking" was listed as a favorite activity on almost every fish profile she had reviewed. I hadn't considered this before, but Vicki was right. Being more oriented toward action sports, I have often challenged whether "hiking" could even qualify as an activity. The very word *activity* stems from the word *active* so by my definition walking in a scenic location shouldn't qualify as an activity any more than walking around downtown would.

Vicki and I skipped our pedicure the next Saturday morning and headed to the appointed trailhead to take the first hike either of us had been on in years.

A three-mile hike should be a no-brainer for someone like me who spends half-an-hour of every day walking uphill on the treadmill as part of my daily workout, and only two years earlier completed an eight-mile, uphill mountain climb as part of my ALF fellowship training. Still, we hadn't walked a quarter-mile when we took our first break. Then we decided to stop every quarter mile, and soon the stops became longer and the steps became shorter, and it took us considerably longer than the estimated hiking time of one hour posted on trailhead signage.

"This is harder than I thought," said Vicki, when she got the breath to talk on our sixth or seventh break, and I agreed. Of course, it might have been different if we had worn the correct shoes for this activity, and water bottles would have been helpful too. Being the urbanites we are, accustomed to walking all over the downtown in heels all day every day, we saw this little three-mile jaunt as something we could easily do in flip flops – and both had assumed a park within the city limits would have drinking fountains along the trail and probably bathrooms too, and we were wrong on both counts.

Vicki and I eventually hit our stride, partly by refraining from conversation when we were walking and also by channeling the foot pain and dry throat into something more productive: fish antipathy. On each of our frequent stops we would each share a story of a particularly foul fish we had been thinking about: I focusing my bitterness on the recently departed Mike4, and Vicki choosing to vent about the man who wanted to go on this hike – a fish she had not yet laid eyes on. We ran out of fish to complain about on the last break, so we chatted venomously about a local politician we were both in vehement disagreement with instead.

When we finally reached the pinnacle it was worth the aching thirst, blistered feet, and general disgust with men. The entire valley was spread out before us, and the downtown we had come from looked like a storybook village on the horizon. Already breathless from the hike, we were also speechless when we saw how much altitude we had gained in three miles, and the sheer magnificence of the view.

"Wow," said Vicki, "the pond looks pretty big from this vantage point."

I agreed and quietly marveled at how many Mikes there probably were in this vast sea of houses and buildings, and how many of the garages held very rare Harley Davidsons of all kinds and colors. I wondered how many of these houses contained families and how many were occupied by one single person. I imagined the internet "tubes" connecting all these houses and buildings together, and wondered how many people were having virtual conversations with each other at that moment, and I voyeuristically mapped out where they would meet for coffee when they connected. I don't know if Vicki was thinking the same thing, but we were both uncharacteristically quiet for a good long while.

We got home and applied first aid to the blisters between our toes, because walking downhill in flip flops is really hard on that particular part of the foot, and realized we would probably have to miss a few pedicures waiting for the wounds to heal. Vicki bought hiking boots for her hike with a fish on the following Saturday, and afterward said it was easy the second time around with bottled water and the proper footwear.

I updated my profile to include "hiking" to my list of activities, and started perusing the pond for men not named Mike who share my passion for walking uphill in a scenic location. There were a few, and one wanted me to ride to the trailhead on the back of his *very rare Harley*, to which I agreed. However I get there, I will get there, because looking at the Valley from atop the highest peak is my new drug of choice. Every once in a while it is uplifting to see how a million people live together in relative peace; to be reminded that our pond is vast and plentiful; and to see that I live in a storybook village, in which one can only live a fairy tale life.

19

Polyamory

My fourth-grade teacher added a postscript to my report card at the end of the school year noting my exceptional vocabulary for a nine-year-old. Never wishing to lose that distinction, I kept a dictionary close at hand for years so if I came across a new word, I could look it up and put it into use immediately. Now I find myself losing many of the words that once impressed my fourth grade teacher and have Wikipedia book-marked on my laptop, which I often consult when reading *Plenty-of-Fish* profiles.

Considering *Plenty of Fish* is a dating site for lay people, it is surprising how much sociological termi-nology is used on the site. And considering I am a human social relationship scholar, it is humiliating how often the terminology stumps me. I got an email once from a fish dressed like Marilyn Monroe who self-identified as a "transgendered anatomically male heterosexual." I had to think about it for a minute, before guessing that he/she was like a lesbian with a penis. I like to be open-minded about people's sexual orientation, but I swing pretty straight in that regard and threw Marilyn back.

I had not heard the term "pansexual" before I started fishing either. Thanks to Wikipedia, I learned that pansexuals could be attracted to people of all genders, which can mean men, women; transgendered men and women; gay men and gay women; and even Catholic Priests. (OK, I added the last one, because the Wikipedia definition says people of all sexual orientation, which I assume could include celibate males.) So the self-proclaimed pansexual who took my bait was released quickly when I got a mental picture of him hitting on a priest and hitting on a nun at the same time.

It's all very confusing to the uninitiated, but fish come in many sizes, shapes and colors.

One day I had a fish in my livewell named Ted who was looking very perfect. Cute profile photo... age appropriate... interesting job... Ivy League education... shared interests... check, check, check, check. All was looking good until I started reading his profile. In the first sentence of perfect Ted's essay he set the stage for what he was looking for: *I am Polyamorous, and looking for women of the same mindset.* He then went on to list the usernames of other women on *Plenty of Fish* with whom he was in polyamorous relationships.

My initial reaction was to roll my eyes and move on, but I consulted the wiki-wizards anyway just to reacquaint myself with the freakish, oppressive human behavior over which I was superior. It seems I was thinking of Polygamy, in which a man could have multiple wives and girlfriends, but the arrangement was not reciprocal and the women could not bring additional husbands into the compound. Polyamory is much different from that. *Poly* - from the Greek word meaning *several*, and *amor*, from the Latin word for *love*, put together simply means "many lovers." And, according to Wikipedia, the most distinctive difference between polyamory and just plain screwing around is the presence of consent, openness and a level of commitment.

This explains why Ted felt the need to identify himself as polyamorous, and then to list the Pollys he is amorous with. An interesting concept, and a refreshingly honest profile, I thought.

Then it hit me: I AM polyamorous! There is a word for me, and what I am doing, and it is a word I should embrace immediately. It perfectly describes the Holly Golightly state of mind I am in: open for romance, but not ready for another marriage or even a serious dating relationship. Polyamory. Even the word sounds exotic, yet intelligent, and I couldn't wait to start using it.

To think that I – a woman educated in the science of human social relationships – was using the wrong phrase to describe the stage I was in. I would tell people I was "single and dating" which would always lead to a discussion about what I was looking for, and why I wasn't finding it. No one in my world was getting the concept of fishing just to fish, and not as a prelude to having fish for dinner. They just didn't see me as the sport-fisherman type, and on that I would agree.

"Single and dating" describes someone who is single, but doesn't want to be; dating to assess the compatibility of various candidates for the position of soul mate or life partner so they won't have to be single anymore. The very term "dating" sounds like a test-run, whereas "relationship" connotes permanence. So people who are dating are thought to be on test-drives for something more permanent. Who says people cannot just date for an indefinite number of years, and that a relationship can't be committed and serious, but not exclusive, and perhaps only for a couple of weeks or months? I think the polyamorous are on to something.

There are men that I keep going out with because I like spending time with them, yet I keep fishing because I don't see soul mate potential in any of these men. Now that I am entering my second year sans-husband, I am less and less certain that I am looking for another serious, committed, monogamous, long-term relationship again; at least not for a while.

So I changed my profile to read: *Polyamorous hetero-sexual female looking for men of same or similar mindset.* Now I believe my intentions are crystal clear. I can finally stop spending the first half-hour of every coffee date stammering through my lame answer to the inevitable question: "What is it you're looking for?"

I am looking for love, but until I find it, I am not limiting myself to the companionship of only one person. I am not deceptive by nature, so cheating doesn't suit me. Becoming polyamorous means that everyone will know about each other and that everyone has approved the arrangement. And I want us to all be friends... and I want us to be honest and to communicate... and I am imagining the need for an on-line dating calendar all of my paramours can have access to... and maybe there could be an annual picnic of my paramours and their paramours... and I am completely dreaming, because the fish I know all want to think they are the center of my universe.

All of the men I have dated made it abundantly clear they do not want to know there are others. I am in two long-distance relationships to men who both say they don't want to know IF I am dating other men. *If?* Do they think I am satisfied with their infrequent swoops in to town, and that they are providing enough of a social life to sustain me? Even globetrotting Prince Charming from Great Britain took issue with the thought of there being others. The prince and I had only one date (on which he bit me) and then a year of phone calls, yet he referred to me throughout that year as his "girlfriend."

Which begs the question: who are these polyamorous people, and are they really all completely cool and consenting? I went back to Ted's profile and noticed then that his list of poly-paramours included the phrase NOT OK WITH IT after two of the user-names. The plot thickens. So I sent Ted an email saying I was also polyamorous, and suggested we chat. His response came a few days later (polyamory leaves one with little time for fishing, I assume) and he was eager to meet.

The coffee date with Ted was different from most coffee dates, in that he wanted to know first and fore-most about all the other men in my life. Then he asked me what was lacking with each of them that I felt the need to keep fishing. I started to answer, when it occurred to me that Ted was sounding like a traditional, possessive male and not the highly evolved, polyamorous human he proclaimed to be.

"Why does something need to be *lacking* in these men for me to keep fishing?" I asked. Ted said he was simply trying to assess whether I was truly polyamorous, or just gasping for air to keep from drowning in a sea of fish. He had a point. I needed to give this more thought.

Ted was a true and committed Poly (as he called himself) in that his relationships were not fleeting and sordid, but long term and committed. There were just more of them than our society would deem acceptable. He pointed out that the whole cornerstone of Polyamory is admitting you need, and can handle, more relationships in your life than just one, and said once he had reached that level of acceptance there was no need to end one relationship in order to embark on another. "Polyamorous relationships typically last longer than the average serial-monogamous relationship," he claimed.

This is all fascinating to me, so I continue to fire questions at him. I wondered if Polyamory and "Swinging" were essentially the same thing, and Ted – with unexpected seriousness – explained that the differences were vast. Swingers, he said, were couples that were true to each other emotionally, but not sexually. And there were many rules governing the swing set. There could be no contact before or after a sexual encounter, for example. You could have sex at a swing party if your significant other consented, and sometimes only in the open where others at the party could observe. Everyone at a swing party was there by invitation of the host – the theory being that everyone was selected for their attractiveness as a sex partner – so all in attendance would have sex with someone, or everyone, at some point in the night. (This is good to know, anecdotally, because I always lamented the thought of showing up at a swinger's party wherein no one expresses interest in me.)

Ted said he had explored "the lifestyle" at one point but found it to have too many rules. It didn't take a rocket scientist to see that Ted didn't like rules. "Polyamory is not as much about sex, but about relationships," he continued. He claimed to love every one of his poly-paramours, and felt no need to cut one loose to make room for another. Again, there's a level of commitment. "What swinging and polyamory have in common – which distinguishes both groups from the more common practice of serial monogamy – is the need to clarify the distinction between relationships and sex, with each group setting different limits on the extent of emotional involvement," he explained.

After a few hours with Ted – which moved from a coffee shop to a bar, because I needed vodka for this conversation – I became more and more enthralled with polyamorous ideology.

Much the way a gay or a bisexual child knows at an early age they are different from their contemporaries, the polyamorous learn at an early age that conforming to social norms will present a problem. Ted said he knew in high school the jealousy he would hear other teens expressing angst over was a completely foreign concept to him.

"I was dating Karen, and then I asked Susan out for a date, and then I asked Margie to the prom, but suggested that we go with Karen, Susan and their respective dates to dinner beforehand," Ted explained. "Karen, Susan and Margie responded to my suggestion by calling me names and publicly defacing my locker, and I didn't end up going to the prom or seeing Susan and Karen again either. I didn't get it. I couldn't comprehend why this was a problem. I liked going to movies with Karen, because we both liked horror films. Susan was my debate partner, and I could converse with her for hours. Margie was a good friend, and I knew she really wanted to go to the prom. Why was I being chastised and ridiculed for wanting to make all of these girls – each of whom I liked very much – happy?"

And it wasn't one-sided.

"I couldn't grasp the concept of male possessive-ness either. I would hear boys in the locker room talking about wanting to kick a guy's ass for talking to his girlfriend; and I couldn't understand the reasoning. If your girlfriend likes this other guy, and you profess to love the girlfriend; then why wouldn't you look at this other guy as someone you had a lot in common with? My inclination was to befriend someone like that."

So the most basic precept of polyamory is the complete absence of jealousy or possessiveness. This is sounding more and more attractive to me, as I have always abhorred possessive men, and I have never been the jealous type either.

My date with Ted went from coffee, to drinks, to dinner and he insisted on paying for everything. To be polyamorous and chivalrous would seemingly get very expensive. I couldn't help but be impressed.

It seems Ted could afford to be polyamorous. He tried to explain to me what he did for a living, but lost me when it started to sound like math. All I gleaned from his explanation is that he was the CTO (which everyone in Silicon Valley knows is an acronym for Chief Technology Officer) for a company that makes *thingamajiggys* communicate with *techno bobbles*, and somehow because they were communicating I am able to change the color of a bathing suit in the Victoria's Secret catalogue without the model needing to change clothes. (I am sure there are more life-altering applications for his company's technology, but the color and pattern-changing capability of on-line shopping is the "killer app" that got my attention in recent years.) Ted was a well-paid genius, and you should love a man with money who chooses to spend his money supporting women. Lots of women, it would seem.

When I got home from my marathon date with Poly-Ted I went straight to my livewell, eager to see how my proclaimed polyamory had improved my haul of fish for the day. I had one email suggesting I attend a swinger's party, and another calling me a pervert. Yet another email was from a married man who claimed to be polyamorous but said his wife didn't know, which defies the poly principle of openness. It was clear the vast majority of fish in the pond was not familiar with the term, and did not consult Wikipedia for clarification.

This was not the outcome I was looking for. I would need to consult Ted for guidance as to what I was doing wrong. But Ted was leaving for the east coast in the morning to spend a few weeks with the mother of his infant daughter. And then he would be in the mid-west for another week with one of his common-law wives before heading to India to check in on one of his overseas programming teams, which most likely included at least one or two additional paramours.

I would have to wait a month to get another counseling session with my new mentor. Damn.

A month between dates – hmmm. Is this what polyamory is really about? So many love interests it would take a secretary to keep schedules straight? There are logistical considerations to this new way of thinking which need more careful consideration. Do I have the time for polyamory, considering I barely find time for one fish date a week? Could I keep track of conversations when I am having so many? How often do the polyamorous get tested for STDs? And most importantly, am I attractive and desirable enough for many to love me in the tiny allotment of time I could spare each fish?

Ted doesn't seem to have a problem in this regard. He is sweet, honest, interesting, humble, considerate, smart, funny and huggable. If he were a fish – and it's easy to forget that he *is* a fish – Ted would be a sushi-grade Ahi Tuna: Tasty enough to eat raw, complex enough to satisfy with only a sushi-sized bite or two, and so abundant it would be selfish not to share.

20

The Fish Who Got Away

Before we both started Internet dating, I could count on my business partner and one-time roommate Mike to be my male companion on those occasions when I didn't have a date, and was overdosing on estrogen. I could always find a girlfriend to spend time with, or talk to, and my evenings were sometimes booked for drinks with women every night of the week right after I became single. Every once in a while, though, I would find myself missing the smell of testosterone, and the unsupportive, shallow repartee one can only get when talking to a man. For me, that man was Mike.

Mike and I lived together right after our respective marriages ended, which I suppose requires some explanation. I was still married to one business partner, when the other (Mike) told us about his recent separation, and said he was living in a cheap motel. I offered our guest room to him while he figured out his next move, not knowing then my own husband was planning to leave in a few days. Whether it was a strange coincidence, a conspiracy against me by my business partners, or something in the coffee at the office I will never know for sure. Over time I came to think of it as a karmic reward.

At first it was awkward having Mike in the house when my marriage was falling apart, and it raised a few eyebrows with the neighbors and some of our employees when they noticed a shift in the principals' carpool routine. But there was never anything between Mike and me, except we became closer friends during that time, and I don't know how I would have coped without him. He was never home, and really didn't provide much support, but I liked knowing there were still two adults living in the monster house with Travis. It gave me a sense of still being a family, even if the family was never home.

The roommate arrangement lasted for six months, during which time we made a pact: I would be his girl when necessary if he would be my boy. This was a practical arrangement made when I realized I was incapable of operating power tools, opening jars, and lifting heavy boxes, and he was incapable of selecting sheets to fit a bed. So we helped each other set up our respective single residences, and I got to furnish not one - but two - new apartments, and he spent more than a few Saturdays moving furniture from the house to the apartment we lived in for a month, until he finally helped get me settled in my fishbowl.

My relationship with Mike started as professional. He joined our agency as Creative Director about ten years earlier, and we made him a partner after five. Besides working together and living together, Mike and

I share a passion for top-shelf vodka and lowbrow drinking establishments. As luck would have it, one day they opened a little place called *Dive Bar* across the street from our office. The two of us would treat ourselves to a drink when we had just finished conceiving a great campaign for a client, or to help ideas flow when we weren't terribly inspired; and the whole staff would often end the week at *the Dive* for "Ketel One Fridays." Sometimes Mike and I could be found at the Dive for karaoke on Wednesdays too. Mike liked to sing Sinatra, and my only song was *These Boots are Made for Walking*, which I guess is a Sinatra song too, so we called ourselves the Sinatras.

The fact that Mike and I were friends surprised a lot of people, since we would get in terrible fights at the office that would last for weeks and sometimes months. He could offend me much more than any of my female friends; and it would seem I rubbed him the wrong way all too often as well. The pattern would often repeat: Mike would blow me off when I was upset or emotional; and thought I was over-reaching or butting in when I gave him unsolicited personal advice. Lisa once observed that Mike treats me like a guy and I treat him like a girl, which explained a lot of the turmoil in our relationship.

Guys don't give each other advice and don't ask for advice. If a guy is going through some kind of emotional upheaval, he stays away from his friends and processes the situation in solitude. Women are the opposite of that. We process things out loud, together, and define the depth of our friendships by the extent to which we can disclose personal information without judgment.

So Mike and I would get into the kinds of fights husbands and wives get into, but without the benefit of make-up sex. And yet we had a stronger bond than sex, in that we relied on each other for our very livelihood. Good creative directors are hard to find, and I was not about to lose the best strategic partner I had ever worked with over something petty and personal, which is usually what our arguments were about. Learning to communicate with Mike was key to our company's survival.

On more than one occasion, Mike would have to remind me he is not my *girlfriend*, like when I asked him once if I looked good after a haircut. Before we learned to communicate, I would be hurt when his answer was "I dunno, I don't look at your hair, ever." Later he learned to answer any question about my appearance with "I'm a guy," and the conversation about my female insecurity was over.

Every married couple could learn from our experience. All the fights, and the long talks that ensue when we're trying to work things out, is how Mike came to be one of my closest friends. If only I had worked that hard at my marriage.

It was my idea for Mike to jump in the pond with us. He had only dated one woman since his marriage ended, and she had just asked for a break. It wasn't a great relationship, but I knew he would beg her back after a month or so if he didn't get laid soon, because I know Mike and – like most men – his behavior is fairly predictable. Becoming a fish in the pond seemed to me a good way for Mike to splash around and gain back some confidence. He resisted at first, but curiosity and physical need got the best of him. Two days after I made the suggestion, he showed up in my livewell just to say hello.

Mike only has two or three nights a week free for anything besides his three boys, and he filled every one of them with fish dates. When he made fish dates for Wednesday nights and Friday nights, and arranged to meet them at *our* Dive Bar, I joked that he would not have time for me anymore. Soon it wasn't a joke. He did not have time for anything but fishing. I had created a monster – a sea monster that could not thrive on dry land.

I was jealous of Mike because he seemed to have so many more choices than I did, which was ridiculous when I think about it because my livewell is full enough, but nothing about female insecurity is rational. Were there more women than men in the pond, or is Mike a more attractive catch than I am? Molly noted that women are more aggressive than men when it comes to fishing, as they are perpetually in a life-long search for a soul mate and it is always their priority. As an amateur sociologist, I have many theories on this, and they all center on those fairy tales ending with capturing the heart of the leading man and living happily ever after. (Fairy tales are now called "chick-flicks," and women watch more than they should.)

The funny thing about Internet dating is this: I

have replaced Mike a few times over now with fish. I haven't made a love connection with anyone, but I have turned two or three fish into really nice male friends who I can talk to when I need that hit of testosterone and the plain talk that goes with it. So at this point, Mike is kind of redundant. But fishermen always pine for the one that got away, so I sigh as Mike swims further and further out to sea, until one day he had vanished. After four months of Internet dating, Mike was caught. All his talk about not wanting to commit is abandoned, and he left the pond for dry land and a steady girlfriend.

One less fish to fry – as I see it now – because as much as I tried to think of him as something like a girlfriend, Mike really was just a fish. Men can't be girlfriends no matter how hard you try. In the movie *When Harry Met Sally,* the basic premise was that men and women couldn't be friends because "the sex thing" always got in the way. Billy Crystal's character said that men are always thinking about having sex, and it prevented them from ever looking at a woman as anything but a future, a potential, or a not-in-a-million-years-but-I-can-dream sex partner. Mike once told me that in his mind there was fun-fun, like getting together with friends; and there was *fun-fun*, which ended with sex. That was how he explained why a fish date would always take precedence over hanging out with me.

I never had to worry about the sex thing getting in the way of my friendship with Mike. The fact that we were both single and both looking, and never looking at each other would – on occasion – fill me with irrational self-doubt. Once at the Dive Bar, after I had consumed more vodka than planned, I got kind of sentimental with Mike and put my arm around him in a "you're my pal" kind of way, to which he jerked away from me like I had body odor. Another time I was telling him about a really bad fish date I had been on and tried to explain my definition of a horrible kiss. When he didn't get it, I said, "let me show you" and planted a very bad kiss on his lips. He wiped his mouth, pushed me away, and said "Eeeeeew YUCK."

Granted, it was a very bad kiss, but when a man pushes you away in disgust after you've made oral contact, it sticks in your head for a while. Made me feel like an old woman who just tried to slip the tongue to her grandson. Creepy. *Lock me up before I kiss again!*

So there was never any doubt in my mind that the mere thought of having a physical relationship with me was pretty repulsive to Mike, so "the sex thing" never got in the way of our friendship or our professional relationship, which was always strong and unwavering. After we both started fishing, and I saw his rigid age requirements, I came to see that I was many years older than what he considered to be touchable. And the girlfriend he just broke up with could have been my daughter. So my friend was an ageist, and I am the creepy grandmother, which is funny to me only because I wasn't trying to date him on-line.

Girlfriends will prop me up when I need it; say I look great when I don't; convince me the rest of the world is wrong, even when it isn't true; and can pull me out of the black hole when I'm depressed. Mike was never good for any of that. And as many times as we were out drinking together, or home drinking together when we were roomies, there never once came a time we even came close to stumbling into bed together by accident, through bad judgment induced by alcohol, or out of sheer need; never once.

So, I guess for me the sex thing did get in the way. For Mike it was something much different. To him, I represented the work and responsibility he needed to get away from at the end of the day. He said he reached a point where he saw me too much and didn't want to hang out with me anymore, even before he disappeared into the pond. Being around me just reminded him of the smaller client budgets and leaner staff, and all the ensuing frustrations in trying to keep the Agency viable in a depressed economy. Not ironically, that was one of the many reasons my soon-to-be-ex-husband said he wanted to get away from me in his "you're great, but I'm leaving" speech.

Herein lies the reason one should not marry a business partner, and should not be good friends with them either. Work is work. Family is family. Girlfriends are girlfriends. Boyfriends are boyfriends. Fun is fun, and *fun is fun*. It's amazing how much better work flowed at the office when the blurry lines between professional and personal relationships became sharp and defined – not unlike my taste in men.

21

Fishing Economics

The economic downturn of 2008-2010 affected everyone I know, but some more than others. Three of my close friends lost houses in foreclosure, and everyone who was not self-employed became unemployed at least once during that period of time. Those of us with businesses saw revenues drop to depths we didn't think possible, and plans for early retirement were put on hold indefinitely.

There was a time when I thought people who had their houses snatched back from the bank were irresponsible. Now, it is to be expected that anyone who bought real estate between 2004 and 2008 will end up in a short sale or in foreclosure. It would be foolish to hold on to a house worth half of its mortgage, so handing it back to the bank became the prudent thing that responsible people would do in this situation.

It is on the heels of this downwardly mobile time in American history that I started fishing. My income was down about 60 percent, and my business isn't worth a red cent, even if there were someone out there with the cash to buy a business. While I abhor the existence of gold-diggers – as they completely undermine all the work we did as feminists in the 1970s – somewhere in the back of my mind I can't help but fantasize about meeting a rich man who will dig me out of this financial hole I'm in, so I won't have to do it with my own shovel.

I am enough of a realist to know this is highly unlikely. Not only are there no rich guys left on the planet, but fishing in "Recently Divorced Lake" is hardly the place to catch one.

A fish I met named Gary seemed well heeled, judging from his car and his clothes, but spent most of our coffee date grilling me on my financial stability. He said most of the women he met on-line were gold-diggers, and he was just not willing to give half of his wealth to a woman again. After he settled with his Cougar ex-wife, Gary started seeing her 28 year-old boyfriend traveling around in a brand new Ferrari with vanity plates proclaiming the driver to be "MYBABY." Ouch.

I wasn't looking for a sugar daddy or a "mybaby," but my Dunn & Bradstreet rating did not measure up under Gary's scrutiny. So in effect - it was he who had become the gold-digger. Either way, there was not a second date.

So most of the fish I met on-line in 2011 had just seen their net worth drop by half in the economic downturn, and then drop by half again through the division of assets with an ex. Therefore, the few remaining men who had enough money to bail me out and restore me to my former self were absolutely and completely unwilling to do so. And who could blame them?

My measure of a man's worth is significantly more weighted toward character than prosperity now. If I had been fishing in the 1990s or pre-2008, I would have been quick to dismiss as a boyfriend candidate someone who told me on the first date he had just filed for bankruptcy and moved in with his parents to save money. Not now. In today's world, I view survival skills as the sign of a smart, successful man. Having a job, any job or income, is the upward-mobility I now find attractive.

Considering my seriously impacted paycheck, dating three or four nights a week sometimes is how I make ends meet. While it flies in the face of my feminist values, I quietly exhale a sigh of relief every time a fish picks up the check without discussion. It's been a difficult transition from feminist to *femme fatale*, but I have actually come to depend on chivalry.

Mike and I had many conversations about the economics of dating. There were times when he had to cancel a fish date because he simply couldn't afford to take a woman out in the manner he saw fit. As my business partner, Mike and I are in the same financial rut, except he still supports a stay-at-home wife and three children. And then there are the multiple fish-dates he paid for, including those with women who grossly overstated their qualities in their on-line profile. Ouch again.

I think of Mike – and guys like Mike – every time one of my fish picks up the check, and hope my acceptance of this charitable act is not causing a child to go hungry somewhere in the primary home. I feel a little guilty too, and hope my date thinks my company worthy of the expense. When I didn't hear from Gary again I wondered if it had to do with the numerous things we didn't have in common, or the fact that I made no effort whatsoever to reach for the check. But I'm getting better at accepting charity.

A fish named Ryan was one of those men of character who met me for coffee one day. He had been a big fish in the industry most impacted by the economic downturn: real estate development. As he told me the story of the housing subdivision he had just broke ground on in September of 2008, I stopped listening. I already knew how it would end because I'd heard this story too many times before. The phrase "You had me at hello" could be replaced with "You had me at – *in September of 2008 I had just...*"

So I focus instead on the survival details. I am looking for the happy ending, or a sign there will be a happy ending, because I am in no position to support a MYBABY. In Ryan's case it looked like he would land back on his feet by selling sofas at his family's furniture store. His goal was eight couches a day, which was fairly easy for a motivated guy to do. To truly restore himself financially though, Ryan would need to sell at least eight couches and three dining sets a day, seven days a week.

For Ryan to be on this coffee date with me, and still make his quota, meant he would work late into the night to make up for the time away from the showroom. While I love a hard working man, and Ryan impressed me with his survival skills and character, there seemed to be no way a relationship with someone who worked 12-hour days, seven days a week could work. Ryan deserved to be someone's MYBABY, and I sincerely hope he finds her.

Vicki agreed to meet a particularly persistent fish with a blue-collar job, reasoning that he had a job, and spelled all the words in his email correctly. "I guess I shouldn't think of myself as too high and mighty to date a forklift operator," she said, pointing out that I had enjoyed my date with the furniture salesman.

In the days leading up to her coffee date, Vicki and I romanticized this forklift operator named Tony, all based on his superb ability to spell the word "beautiful" correctly. Maybe he's a poet or a sculptor, or some kind of an artist who supports his art with manual labor? Perhaps he's an astronomer who could only see the galaxy at night, and did physical work during the day to allow his brawn to earn a living, while his brain processed astrological discoveries? We couldn't wait to find out.

A few minutes into the coffee date, Vicki discovered that Tony was none of those things. He was only a forklift operator, and a not very pleasant one at that. When he learned Vicki's son Jeremy was a lawyer, he asked for free legal counsel to defend him against a sexual harassment complaint against him. He also mentioned pending lawsuits against his landlord, his auto mechanic, and the veterinarian he believed had killed his dog. Reviewing legal briefs is probably how Tony had learned to spell big words.

Survival skills are admirable, but litigiousness will not be tolerated. So Tony was released, and Vicki and I both resumed the practice of screening fish by profession. I released a truck-driving fish, a fish-janitor, and even a fish living off his father's lucrative patent. The latter surprised a few of my friends, since a patent-holder would be the most likely candidate for a financial savior, but I have this need to date people who have jobs. What else is there to talk about?

The closest I got to economic relief from dating is when my poly-friend Ted invited me to live with him rent-and-mortgage-free at his ranch in Woodside. He offered me the room next to the horse stables, with its own bathroom, and told me I could get my own horse if I wanted one. Would this cushy arrangement make me a "kept" woman? Perhaps, but one has to assume a Poly household would have many female inhabitants, so the pressure on me to "service" the landlord would not be terribly tiresome, and there would always be women to talk to.

It's good to know I have a place to go in the event the real estate market takes another downward turn and I am forced to give my fishbowl back to the bank. I know I possess the survival skills to keep myself afloat, but I am starting to question my own character.

I will consider this offer from Ted to be Fallback Plan B. (Maybe C.)

22
Fishing On Dry Land

As prolific as Mike was as a fish, the woman he ended up in a committed relationship with was not someone he met on-line. He met her in a bar. Still, he would never have met her at all if it weren't for *Plenty of Fish*, and it was an Internet date on which they met. Mike had been chatting with a fisherman who lived in San Francisco, but she was reluctant to date anyone who lived more than 20 miles away, because she had just ended a long-distance relationship and was looking for someone closer to home. Mike liked everything about her (which means he thought she was hot) so he persisted until she finally acquiesced and agreed to a meeting.

Knowing this was going to be a hard sell, and wanting to impress this fine fisherman, Mike made reservations at a nice restaurant in San Francisco for their first date. The meeting was a disaster. This wiggler who lured Mike into her livewell had used a lot of tricky lures to do so, and was nothing at all what her profile represented. First, she had posted a picture of her younger, slimmer sister instead of one of her own, and was quite a bit older than Mike, and not aging well. The "few extra pounds" she was carrying were not in good places, he told me when relaying the story to me the next day, and they found very little to talk about. "No chemistry and no conversation value," he said, calling it "a money and time-wasting combination."

Once dinner was over, Mike used the excuse of an early morning meeting to exit the restaurant before the waiter came back to see if they wanted dessert. Once on the street, and seeing his date drive away, he popped back into the restaurant and took a seat at the bar. He needed a stiff drink to calm his nerves after his disappointing date. Only a sip or two into his martini, an attractive, age-appropriate woman took the seat next to him and they started talking. Her name was Melissa, and it seems she had just escaped a disastrous Internet date of her own. Mike and Melissa stayed in the bar until closing time, and told each other their respective life stories. By the time they exited to the street, they were both too drunk to drive home so they checked into a nearby hotel. The next day they both disabled their *Plenty of Fish* profiles. So Mike met his soul mate in a bar, which is a perfectly respectable place to meet someone in my opinion.

When I hear stories like how Mike met Melissa it makes me wonder if the inherent lack of alcohol is the reason I haven't met "Mr. Right" on the Internet. I am a better person with vodka – ask anyone – and it's the same handicap that caused me to blow many job interviews.

Dead sober I am riddled with self-doubt and nervous jitters. One or two vodka tonics with a *splash o' cran* and I am confident, happy, fun to be around, and – perhaps most important in this context – beautiful. Yes, it's true: alcohol makes me better looking. You've heard of beer bottle lenses? Well, they work in the mirror too.

Looking back, I now realize that every serious relationship I have been in was kindled in an alcohol-induced state. My first husband and I went to high school together. Years of smiling at each other in the halls and telling friends we liked each other did nothing to put a class ring on my finger. But two years after graduation we met again in a bar and it took less than 10 minutes and three or four beers to realize we had mutual, mad crushes on each other throughout our teen years and were, therefore, fated to be together as adults.

Husband number two worked with me at a large New York ad agency, and we rode the elevator together to the 42nd floor nearly every day for a year with not so much as a word exchanged. It took the company Christmas party and lots of - *duh* - alcohol before he was proclaiming his deep, unspoken admiration for me and I was confessing to finding him the best looking man, with the cutest butt, at the company. In *Vodkian*, the real language of love, that translates into "I have found my soul mate."

The third and most recent stroll down the aisle 20 years ago would never have taken place if we had only served together on that event committee. No. It took the event itself, and the post-event committee celebration at... *drum roll please*... a bar, for us to get together. That same husband met his first girlfriend Marina in a bar too. I can't imagine how *that* could have happened without alcohol. (I am still puzzled as to how it happened even WITH alcohol, but I have my soon-to-be-ex-husband's word that some day he will tell me the story.) Who would chat up a married man having dinner with his family? Yes, his family: Travis, me, and my parents celebrating (ironically) Father's Day. He went to settle the bar tab after we got seated for dinner, and came back with a phone number in his pocket. I know, because I do his laundry. (I mean I *did* his laundry at the time.)

So, please, all you people who say things like "Well, it's better than meeting men in bars," when you're speaking of Internet dating, have not heard the tale of Mike and Melissa.

Another common phrase, usually uttered as justification for fixing me up with a single neighbor, widowed co-worker, or permanently single-for-a-reason relative, is:

"Do you know what kind of men you meet in bars? Drunks!"

Yes, drunks. Good drunks, happy drunks, talky drunks, handsome drunks. Gotta love the drunk men! They seldom ask questions or make judgments. They just think I am incredibly beautiful (because I AM with vodka), and we talk about silly things we have in common, like agreeing that Prince was more talented than Michael Jackson in the '80s. Soon we mutually determine there is nothing we would rather do for yet another evening than talk to each other about absolutely nothing important again. Then we dance, and we laugh, and we drink, and we fall in love.

I remember each and every one of those drunken encounters fondly, even if the best ones ended in a division of cookware.

Internet dating takes the fun, the spontaneity, and the alcohol out of a tried-and-true mating ritual that has served me well over the years. On an Internet date, you know too damned much about each other before you have that first coffee date. *Coffee date!* Caffeine has the opposite effect of alcohol, just so you know. My nervousness turns into visible shaking which makes it appear as though I suffer from Parkinson's disease. Not that there's anything wrong with people afflicted with Parkinson's, but it's hardly the silky smooth first impression I want to make. And caffeine is as *uglify-ing* as alcohol is *beautify-ing.* How can you "check for chemistry," as we say in the pond, when the chemicals have been tampered with?

I love that spark of excitement I get when I'm sipping on my fourth cocktail and suddenly spot the most handsome man I have ever seen (again, beer bottle lenses) looking my way. I am beautiful, and I know it, so I confidently stare back, smile, and perhaps raise my glass in a flirty air-toast that says - *Yes! You can buy me the next drink, baby.*

He's probably a Republican who hates cats, but all I care about at that moment is how we're going to look together on the dance floor in the photo I will snap of us on my iPhone and send to all my friends to show I am "getting out there." I can almost guarantee a union like this one will last at least one, maybe two months before I even find out he doesn't ski, lives with his mother, and hasn't worked in years. My longest Internet "relationship" lasted only 3 weeks. I've heard of women getting into relationships with bar men they had nothing in common with for a year or more, who said they were wonderful for a month, a year... whatever amount of time it took for the chemistry to wear off and the restraining order to go into effect.

With Mike it was only about chemistry, which is why bars are probably his better hunting ground. He doesn't care much about lifestyle traits, occupation, politics and schedule. He just liked women who could make him smile, and – from the women I have seen him with – had no strong preference for blondes over brunettes, butts over boobs, short versus tall, or any other physical characteristics. Some women just interested him at first glance, and others did not. Even his strict age rules didn't always hold true, as I saw him with a woman once who I am pretty sure was older than me, and Melissa is a year older than him. Pictures can be deceptive, and seldom capture the essence of someone. Mike was disappointed on Internet dates more than any of my friends in the pond, and he probably went on more first dates than any of us in the pond too. I don't think he went on 589 dates like Cindy did, but it's safe to say he ate a lot of worms before getting hooked in a bar. A toast to Mike and Melissa!

My chemistry lesson for today is this: Decent looking, age-appropriate man + alcohol + hormones + bar = relationship. Decent looking, age-appropriate man + coffee + profile + Starbucks = job interview.

Internet dates often do feel a lot like job interviews. "Where do you see yourself in five years?" is a question that always stumped me on interviews and really gets me flustered on coffee dates. Every career counselor will tell you the answer to that question should be "I see myself as a valuable member of your team in five years," or some version of that sentiment. On dates, answering that same question with "married to you, I hope," is a surefire way to scare away a fish.

What is the correct answer to the question on the lips of every fish: "What are you looking for?" I am fuzzy about what I want for the second half of my life, and even more so about a man I have been talking to for 5 minutes, so I blow this question every time. "I'll know it when I see it," is my usual answer, but a lot of fish see this as a form of rejection. I am not talking about him, of course, I am speaking in a Holly Golightly way about knowing I have found the life, and perhaps a man that comes with it, when I wake up one morning and think *this is it.* That same question is never asked in a bar, because people keep conversations light when they are drinking. "What do you want to do now," is a more likely bar question, and the answer is easy – "Let's dance!"

23

Planetary Considerations

In his book *Men are From Mars, Women are from Venus*, Doctor John Gray contends the gender differences between the sexes are so marked that we may as well be from different planets. I agree with the basic contention that men and women view the world – and particularly relationships – very differently. However many men speak Venetian fluently, and there are certain women (such as myself) who could exist pretty well on Mars in the event of a spacecraft mishap too.

Therein lies the basic problem. Every woman knows two or three men who are just as emotional, just as communicative, and just as incapable of fixing things as they are. These are not the men we tend to migrate toward, and many of them are gay, but the very existence of such men tends to lull us into the false belief that all men can be taught to speak Venetian. This is not true.

My soon-to-be-ex-husband spoke Venetian very well for the first ten years of our marriage. The last three or four years, however, he became entrenched on Mars, and conversation became increasingly difficult. He has always maintained a number of close female friends who all find him easy to talk to, so his ability to converse with Venetians is not reserved for intimate relationships. I have always had close male friends too, the closest in recent years being Mike, who speaks not a word of Venetian. My male friendships stem from my need to fix things, which is perhaps my most pronounced Martian tendency, and I seem to come across a lot of men who are in dire need of fixing.

To read the profiles of many fish, one would believe the pond was on the planet of Venus. Many of the men write poetry; claim to enjoy chick-flicks; love sipping wine and enjoying the sunset; think long talks by a fire are a good first date; say they enjoy giving foot massages; and – most notably – love to cook. My assumption on the last item is that men like to eat, and will learn to cook when women stop feeding them. Necessity is the mother of invention, after all, and cooking is all about invention.

Women are deceptive too, but mostly in their pictures. Let's face it; girls learn the tricks at an early age either in charm school or just in the magazines we read. Black is a slimming color and there are ways to stand which accentuate your good side, your good features, and offset the big nose, the not-so-shapely legs, or the flat butt. We learn at an early age how to take a good photo. Men, on the other hand, just capture an image from the camera built in to their computer, or by holding their phone out arm's length and snapping a picture. Chances are it will look like them, but chances are just as good it will be a relatively unflattering photo. This ability to take pictures of oneself is not covered in the Mars and Venus book, so I am not completely clear as to what planetary forces are at play. I just know it's true.

I have also surmised from talking to single women I have encountered in and out of the pond that many of us fisherman are pretty much looking for everything. One woman I met told me she was not willing to settle for anything less than a handsome man with a great body who was smart, successful, and absolutely crazy about her and only her. While I am not usually catty, I could not help but look at this woman critically and surmise that she was not worthy of this perfect man. If she caught one, it would surprise me if he met her last and most important criteria. My experience with perfect men is they require a willingness to share.

To catch a man, you only really need to have one good feature. Trite as it sounds, men are either *ass men* or *boob men* or *face men*. Some say they want "the whole package," but that just means "pretty" in Martian, so a college education is not mandatory.

Vicki speaks Martian very well, but I believe it has more to do with her ability to do things on her own after being single for 25 plus years. She's not masculine in any way, just very independent and logical. Seldom would you see Vicki do something stupid for romantic reasons... at least I thought.

I have only known Vicki to be single, but she has told me stories from her past that prove she can be just as gushy and nonsensical as the rest of the female population under the right influence. There were two great loves in her life - and they were not the two men she married. She has said her first husband – the father of her son Jeremy – was her best friend at the time. Her second marriage lasted 3 months, 18 days and 10 hours - but who's counting?

It seems the first true love of Vicki's life was a married photographer who probably kept her out of a real relationship for nearly 20 years. I learned about David after the third time I helped her move. Molly, Lisa and I were unpacking boxes in Vicki's new living room when we came across a collection of prints: beautiful landscapes of the Illinois countryside; wonderful black and white photos of Jeremy at two or three years old; and probably the best photos of Vicki any of us had ever seen. Vicki decided right then and there it was time to let the world finally see these magnificent prints, and had them framed and matted for display throughout her new condo. This meant coming clean – at least to the girls from the Tail Club who were helping her to unpack – about the photographer/lover who was the reason she left Chicago

Only a few Mondays after we learned about David, Vicki came to the Tail Club with exciting news. Jeremy and his girlfriend Megan were finally getting married. For all her skepticism about the institution of marriage, Vicki was brimming with excitement over the details of Jeremy and Megan's special day. It would be a back-yard wedding held at the home of close family friends. Vicki had pictures of Megan's wedding dress, and several choices for her to wear, all of which needed our collective opinions.

"Have you hired a photographer yet?" asked Kathy, and we all knew where she was going with this question.

"When is the last time you saw David?" asked Mary, to which everyone jumped in to express what a great idea it would be to invite him.

Just what our little group needed to spice things up a bit: our own version of *Mamma Mia* played out right before our eyes, and starring Vicki, who had not been in the middle of a romantic triangle for far too many years.

"Absolutely not," Vicki said, which in Venetian means, "seed is planted, and needs time to sprout." I quietly marveled at the realization that Vicki still spoke a little Venetian. Nothing was said about the Illinois photographer for many months, but there was a lot of discussion at the Tail Club meetings about Jeremy's dad, and whether he would or would not fly out from Chicago to attend his son's wedding.

He did, and David did too. It was a beautiful wedding held on the planet of Venus, and the Martians in attendance did everything they could to keep their planetary tendencies at bay for the day. Vicki and David reconnected, as we all knew they would, and Vicki looked as female and as flirty as I have ever seen her.

Vicki is still one of my closest friends, but she goes home to Chicago more than she used to now. She still keeps a profile on *Plenty of Fish* and talks of coffee dates and fish in her livewell with the rest of us, but I can't help but notice that Vicki is not the skilled fisherman she used to be. Just the other day she mentioned a man she had met on line who seemed perfect in every way, but she blew him off in a cavalier, Venetian way by saying there were plenty more where he came from, and she didn't need one more fish to fry.

I am happy for Vicki, and something about the most jaded fisherman I know reconnecting with the love of her life at middle age gives me small hope for a chick-flick subplot of my own. The Tail Club is getting smaller though, with Vicki and Linda gone so much, Molly dating so prolifically, Lisa back with Seth, Cathy caught on her first coffee date, and the married women getting bored with it all.

I spend more time with fish than I do with girl-friends now, and am beginning to feel is if Venetian is my second language.

NANCI WILLIAMS

24

Fish ON

On-line dating has turned me in to a stalker. I get an email every time someone is looking at my profile, which can suck me back to the pond in the middle of the day, often when I'm busy with real world activity, and even when I'm not in the mood for fishing. It can be very distracting. Imagine you are working away at whatever you do for a living and suddenly a sexy voice whispers in your ear, "Hey, baby, don't stop what you're doing... I am just going to take a few minutes to check you out." I would like to meet the woman who has the discipline to ignore the voice and continue working, since the natural reaction is to stop what you're doing to turn around and see the man behind the sexy voice. The exception to this rule might be a female brain surgeon in the middle of a procedure, but running an advertising agency is definitely not brain surgery.

Once I'm drawn back in the pond I am made aware of everyone else who is on-line at that particular time, and I can't help but wonder why these people don't have better things to do in the middle of the workday than to fish. And as soon as I remember that they all see me there too, I usually log off quickly.

I know when someone is on-line; I know how long he will remain on–line; and I know when he was last on-line. Information may be power, but this kind of information can ruin an otherwise good shot at a relationship.

A fish named Sam was new to on-line dating when we met, so he was a little like a kid in a candy store about the idea of dating a lot of different woman. He hadn't had any bad experiences or disappointing dates as of yet, and – jaded as I was becoming after six months in the pond – I found his enthusiasm for the sport to be kind of sweet. To be honest, I really liked him. Sam was a high-tech executive who had lived in Silicon Valley most of his adult life, and waited until his last daughter was off to college before facing up to the truth of his failed marriage. He was responsible to his family, yet childlike in his enthusiasm for his mid-life crisis. He was a great activity partner, because Sam wanted to go out and do something every night and every weekend, which is unusual for men in mid-life, I have found. He wanted to ski with me, he wanted to rediscover racquetball with me, and I went with him to shop for a motorcycle.

I know enough about human behavior from my sociological studies to understand that a man who is just out of a 30-year marriage to his high school sweetheart is going to need a little time before he settles into a relationship again. I really like Sam and I can wait. I will be the one woman he dates who understands him and knows what he needs to do. I won't push for a commitment before he's ready (and before I'm ready), and I won't give him an ultimatum and demand exclusivity when I learn about other women in his livewell.

I convinced myself that my poly-attitude would serve me well with this fine fish. I would be the fisherman who understands. I would be the one he will talk to and won't have to play games with. I will remain standing when the pettier women give in to their jealous, possessive tendencies, and I will be the one he will call to complain about these other women who don't understand that he needs to go through a process. I am better than all the other nameless, faceless fishermen he may encounter, because I will let Sam be Sam.

And I probably could have done that, and done it just fine, were it not for the stalking tools provided by *Plenty of Fish*.

Sam was on-line ALL THE TIME. Sam would drop me off from what I thought was a great date, and while I was lingering in the afterglow of a perfect evening, he was already back on-line trolling. If I didn't know this, I would have been blissfully ignorant to the fact that this man I had just spent a lovely evening with, and had made me feel completely special, drove home thinking – *tomorrow night* – *the Asian chick!*

On the flip side to Sam's prolific pond behavior was the fact that almost every time he was in the pond for at least an hour or so, he would go to my profile. What a nice feeling to know that someone I have been dating now for several weeks still goes on-line every couple days to look at my profile again. It's kind of like my picture is on his desk, or that I'm his screen-saver. This was the closest I had gotten to feeling like I had a "boyfriend."

Then it came to my attention that Sam let an entire week pass without looking at my profile even once and it drove me to wonder which shiny lure had distracted my fish and whether I would ever hear from Sam again. But I did. I got to where I was checking and re-checking several times a day to see if he had looked at my profile yet, and while I was in the pond checking I could not help but notice that he was there too. It was confusing, because even though Sam stopped looking at my profile, and was always on-line trolling, we were talking and dating pretty frequently. Still, I was beginning to believe that Sam was on-line all the time. He would send me a flirty text message, but instead of just allowing it to make me smile; I would be drawn to my laptop to see if he had sent me the email from the pond. And most of the time my fears would be confirmed. There I would find Sam – fishing, flirting and texting me, all at the same time.

I couldn't stand it anymore, so I took my profile down. No hook in the water, no address in the pond. I decided at that moment to focus my attention on Sam and to do so would require that I remain blissfully unaware of his extracurricular activities.

Four days later I was having dinner with Sam when he mentioned it. "I noticed you took your profile down." Aha! He had finally gone back to my profile, I thought.

"Yes. I did take my profile down," I said, then – not

wishing to make him think I was about to demand exclusivity – added, "I am so busy at work right now, and the pond can be such a distraction."

When he agreed, I just couldn't help myself. I said it. "I did notice that you were on-line a lot of the time."

"Do you have a problem with that?"

"Well, no, I understand that we're not in an exclusive relationship and that you are still playing the field and everything... it's just – that – well – it was just something that I noticed, and wondered why you would go right back on-line after dropping me off from a date."

"You wouldn't know I was on-line unless you were on-line too."

"Yes, but I'm only going on-line to see if you're on-line." Damn! I said it! Now he knows that I stalk him on-line.

"Maybe I'm only on-line to see if you're on-line."

I didn't believe that to be the case, since he used the word "maybe" in his sentence, but I thought it could end this uncomfortable conversation I was having with a man I liked very much, but it only brought us to the inevitable.

"Well, maybe we should both just stop then," I said, immediately wishing I hadn't.

He gave me a heavy sigh and then started in again with the "I'm not ready to be in a relationship" lecture that I had heard on our first, second and third dates.

"No, no," I said, "I'm not like that. I am totally okay with you seeing other women. I understand you, I didn't mean that we should be exclusive, I SO don't need a relationship right now." That was probably enough to end the conversation, but I continued talking anyway. "I was married for 20 years and the last thing I need right now is monogamy," I babbled, "you and I are on the same page, believe me." Then I just couldn't leave well enough alone and continued – "I intend to date every man on *Plenty of Fish* before I settle into a committed relationship, you are just one of many..."

He stopped me and said, "So you're pretty righteous about being a *player* and have no intention of being in a serious relationship? Wow. You must have real self-esteem issues to just collect men with no intention of getting serous about any of them."

Sam had turned the conversation around to being about me. Ouch. I was no longer the understanding poly-girlfriend; now I was a "player" and a slut. I needed to confess to being either an on-line stalker or a relationship-monger to save this date.

I chose the former and admitted to everything. I told him I had taken my profile down because – while I'm fine with him seeing other women – I wasn't comfortable knowing that he was on-line all the time, and was really uncomfortable with getting emails and texts from him while he was trolling on-line. In short, I told the truth. There was a long silence when I was done, and conversation was stilted through the rest of our date. I never heard from Sam again after that night, but I still look at his profile once or twice every week, and can't help but notice that he's ALWAYS on-line.

25
Reflections on the Pond

Perhaps my problem with relationships is this: I never change and *they* always do.

My soon-to-be-ex-husband contends he gave more to our marriage than anything he had done before; that he had stood still longer than he had ever stood still before; and that he had finally changed but I didn't change with him. After all his mid-life transitions, he said he was ready to grow old, to relax; while I seemed to cling to my youth and the way it always was.

I have not changed anything since I was 16 or 17 years old, except for perhaps my weight. I was overweight as a teenager, and managed to get up to 165 pounds and a size 16 by the age of 18. The weight came off naturally over the next two or three years (when I became too busy with college and work to sit at home eating ice cream) but I never stopped seeing myself as overweight. It's called "body dysmorphic," and many women suffer from it. I am 126 pounds and a size 4 today, but I still see a fat teenager when I look in the mirror. The difference at mid-life is that I have been through enough therapy to know I can trust the numbers, but not the reflection, and it's just something I've learned to live with.

The only aspect of my personage that has truly changed over time is my attitude about men and relationships. I am so jaded from seeing three marriages go sour – all to men I was so sure were my soul mate at the time – I don't take anything men say to heart anymore. The net result is I am really bad at taking compliments, and very cynical about romantic rituals.

Fish:	You have beautiful eyes.
Me:	*They're really sensitive to light, and I'm farsighted.*
Fish:	You have a great body.
Me:	*My personal trainer is a guy.*
Fish:	I am really attracted to you.
Me:	*I know... lots of you guys are.*
Fish:	You look great in those jeans.
Me:	*Just in these jeans though. They were pretty expensive.*
Fish:	I'll bet you get a lot of email on *Plenty Of Fish*.
Me:	*Yup. There are lots of fish.*
Fish:	I feel like we are so much alike.
Me:	*My husbands all thought so too in the beginning.*

Fish:	I really appreciate your insights.
Me:	*You'll find them annoying after a while.*

Fish:	I would like to see you again.
Me:	*Figured you would.*

Fish:	I haven't felt this way about someone in a long time, and I... I...
Me:	you *want to have sex with me. Right?*

I'm not callous and insensitive all of the time, but I have to stop myself from laughing at some of the things fish say on dates, when they're not trying to be funny. At my age, romance seems so silly, and mating rituals so trite, I have developed this *been there, done that* attitude toward words and gestures that would have made me tingle all over at a time when I still believed in Beatles song lyrics and happily-ever-after.

I'm too jaded to date; at least that's what one fish told me just before he removed himself from my hook. Maybe I should wait a month between coffee dates so I will at least be a little starved for male attention when I meet a new fish for the first time. But then I remember that it took Cindy 589 coffee dates to meet Jack, and I remember the 600,000 eligible men registered on *Plenty of Fish*, and realize one of them could actually be the soul mate who will make me believe in fairy tales again. Even with my limited ability to process math equations, I can surmise this much: I will still be fishing for *my* Jack at the ripe old age of a-hundred-and-something if I limit myself to only one date a month.

Still, it's hard to put on my game face sometimes when I just don't feel like playing the game. Why am I doing this? What am I fishing for? What is it about my life that is incomplete, and what is the void I am trying to fill? Perhaps it's not a life partner or a soul mate I am fishing for. A few thousand dollars on therapy might reveal that all I'm really seeking is companionship and sex. I am remembering a quote I saw etched in a rock once... something about fishing all your life without knowing it is not fish you are after. I think it was by Henry David Thoreau, and I wonder now if there's some mystical reason I remembered it.

Philosophers, coaches and management consultants always talk about the importance of "visioning." Envision your next move. Imagine your life, your career, and your company in five years, I've been told. Chart your course; set your goals; move forward with a plan... *yadda, yadda, yadda.*

I've never been good with visioning and goal setting in my personal life. I believe in fate and Karma, neither of which can be changed or anticipated. If you believe in fairy tales, then sitting in your window singing "some day my prince will come" will bring his majesty, in all his handsomeness, galloping up to your doorstep with a glass slipper in hand. Some of the fairy tale believers I know say they are very much interested in meeting someone special, but they seldom leave their own home to look for him, and then complain a lot about how lonely it is to be single. I will assume that when they're home alone, they are envisioning their life-ever-after and singing about it in their window at night before curling up with a new romance novel. I would like to see the success statistics on that visioning exercise.

A woman at the health club I go to was telling me about the man she was about to marry – a widower – who she said was exactly the man she had envisioned marrying. Claire suggested that I do what she did: imagine the man I could see myself married to, and promised my dream man would appear. I didn't say it to her, of course, but my mind immediately went to the late wife who had only been gone for a month or two when Claire started dating her husband. If Claire had been "envisioning" this man for years, could it be that she had something to do, inadvertently, with his late wife's untimely death? Could the strength of someone's vision actually succeed in eliminating a life form that stood in the way of reaching a goal? A frightening thought, and one that would make me think twice about settling down with a particularly attractive catch.

There are a lot of holes to the theory of positive thinking, and Indian philosophy makes more sense to me. The doctrine of Karma states that one's position in life is a result of all deeds past, present and future, thus making one responsible for one's own life, and the pain and joy it brings to him/her and others. Since building karma gives me something to do while I await my fate; I guess you could say that's my big life plan.

Everything good in my life has happened because I was in the right place at the right time, or because an action outside of my control set something into motion to my benefit. I honestly believe that when something good happens to me it is my karmic reward for being a good person. My definition of "good" is that I try not to stand in the way of other people reaching their goals and, generally speaking, don't covet the husbands of other women. (Flirt, yes; covet, no.)

Every relationship I have been in was started through happenstance. How could I have planned to be in that bar on the particular day that my future ex-husband was there? At best, I could have made a plan to be in bars or in crowded public places all the time waiting for the moment when a soul mate candidate just so happened to take the seat next to mine, but it would be expensive and unproductive to do so. Still, it's probably closest to the plan I am working from now. *Go out; be social; don't stay home* – is my mantra. There are no interesting, good-looking men living in my fish bowl after all, besides Travis and my cat.

Once I have met someone, I do find some "visioning" exercises to be useful, though. Someone once told me that when you're dating after 50, you have to think in terms of the next relationship being your last relationship: *The bedpan guy.*

Now more than ever, a woman over 50 like me should not settle for anything less than a true, no-compromise soul mate who I would not think twice about... dare I say it... changing his bedpan. More importantly, could I look this man in the eye and say, "Honey, get the bedpan please, I have to go." A sobering thought. The *bedpan guy* consideration is perhaps the most compelling reason I can think of to stay single. I may be independent in a lot of ways, but when I arrive at an age where I can't get myself to the bathroom anymore I hope Travis has the good grace to place me in one of those group homes where there are professionals on hand for bedpan duty.

Maybe I should stay single. My father's mother – the grandmother I never met – was married five times, and her fifth husband killed her one night in a fit of jealous rage. For as long as I can remember I have been likened to the grandmother who was murdered at 41 years of age, whom I supposedly resemble, so staying out of the marriage game may be the best assurance I will live long enough to spend my final days in a home for incontinent senior citizens.

I have been thinking a lot lately about how I am a really good girlfriend, but a lousy wife. A lot of the men I meet say they are looking for someone just like me – independent, opinionated and self-sufficient – but I question their reasoning. Why would someone be attracted to independence, the detritus of co-dependent bliss? A girlfriend who isn't too clingy is one to brag about to the guys at work, but a wife who needs her *alone time* is a threat to the institution of marriage and the American Way.

In a sense then, the very traits men are attracted to in me are the same attributes my husbands wanted to divorce. Again, I don't change. *They* do.

My soon-to-be-ex-husband and I are still business partners, and I see him almost every day. We get along fine now that the drama is over, but I would not characterize him as someone I have a lot in common with today. Still, our 20 year history gives me the familiarity I would need to change his bedpan if he really needed me to, and I like to think he would be willing to return the favor. In his *you're great, but I'm leaving* speech, he gave me credit for always being honest and consistent. He admitted it was *he* who had changed, and it was *he* who had grown weary of my independent ways. I am nothing if not consistent. (Except for the fluctuating weight, of course.)

I went to my high school class reunion a few years ago, and took it as a compliment when people said I hadn't changed a bit. Excepting of course the weight loss, I had to agree that I was pretty much the same person I was in high school. I have another reunion coming up next year, and now wonder if I should mega-mature before I see those people who knew me as a fat teenager again.

Was I supposed to change? If so, when was this transformation supposed to take place? A lot of people I know (men and women) seem to change when they get married. Perhaps my two brief, early marriages screwed me up in that regard? I saw a huge change in my friends after they had children, so not having children of my own may be another factor in my suspended adolescence. Was I supposed to start acting differently when I bought my first house? When I found my first grey hair?

Note to self: *Grow up.*

I am 50 years old, and feel the same as I did in high school. This may not be a good thing; this may not be a healthy mental state of being; and this is definitely not what the big five-oh is supposed to feel like. Besides the Tail Club women – who are all like me – I don't relate to most women my age. When I see women who are supposed to be my age on television or in the movies they are frumpy grandmothers who bake cookies for their adult children, and spend a lot of time reflecting on their past and the future of their grandchildren as if they are already at the end, and not the middle, of their lives. If they are married, they still hold hands with their spouse, because the myth of growing old together in forever-love is still perpetuated by screenwriters who are probably divorced. If the on-screen 50 year-old woman is not married, she is widowed and sad or she is divorced and bitter. I would hardly consider the portrayal of women my age in popular culture to be something I can either relate to or aspire to.

Note to makers of pop culture: *Fifty is not old.*

We baby boomers are expected to live a century or more, so 50-something is the new middle age. People today are waiting until their 30s to get married; starting families in their 40s; and going back to college and starting new careers in their 50s. I don't feel old, I don't see an old person in the mirror every day, and I don't sense the end to anything looming on the horizon. The only thing missing from my life right now, besides a soul mate, is a decent pop culture role model.

Screenwriters should use the Tail Club women to inspire 50-something characters. Kathy with a "K" just left her job as managing partner at a major law firm to be in-house counsel for a non-profit. Molly is playing the best golf of her life, just started singing in a new classic rock cover band, and still stresses about dates as if she were a teenager. Linda finally got the pilot's license she always wanted, and had a fabulous party at the Jet Center when she got her wings. Lisa is going for her third or fourth master's degree – this time in Poetry. Lee, who just went back to teaching at San Jose State University, is one of her professors. Vicki's political consultancy started taking national campaigns this year and opened a satellite office in Chicago. Cathy with a "C" is engaged to be married again, and she managed to start-up a new software company at the same time as she was getting a divorce and falling in love. Suzanne and her husband Jim are shopping for land in Napa Valley to start their own vineyard. Trish was just named CFO of a larger Silicon Valley company, but has future plans to run the tasting room at Suzanne's winery when it opens in eight to ten years.

Since I am not a huge fan of change, I will express my unwillingness to act my age by not changing a thing: I will continue to be consistent; I will continue to be independent; I will continue to go on fish dates, even if I'm too jaded for fishing; and I will continue to ignore the fat teenager in the mirror every day.

26
Danny's Wife

I have now been single long enough to have a past. According to the Tail Clubbers, every man who made it through the coffee date is considered to be one of my exes, and there have been more of those than I like to admit.

I was on the treadmill at the club one day when a familiar-looking man took the machine next to mine and started his run. It took a moment for me to recognize one of the early Mikes, and when I did I had nothing to say. I couldn't remember anything about him, our date, what his assigned number was, or why I had released him. I couldn't even recall whether I *had* released him or he had escaped from my livewell on his own accord. An awkward silence accompanied our simultaneous workout, as I assumed he went through the same mental exercise.

Even more awkward was the ex-fish who called on me one day at work. I couldn't ignore this one, so I sat through his demonstration on a new software product that would make my staff more productive without once making eye contact. I concentrated so intently on the poorly designed PowerPoint slides presented by this fish in a blue suit that my dreams that night were framed in gradated blue bars with scene titles in yellow Helvetica Bold type.

Another time I was walking through the sparkling new terminal at Mineta San Jose International Airport – because my position as past chair of the board of the chamber of commerce got me invited to the grand opening party – when I passed the newsstand and saw a fish I once dated on the cover of a business magazine. One of my exes was a cover-fish! I had to scan the Rolodex in my head before I recalled that this genius fish was released by me for something truly ridiculous: his voice. I remembered having an enjoyable on-line chat with him that started on the Friday lunch hour and continued through the weekend. By Sunday afternoon, we were making plans to meet for coffee, and exchanged phone numbers.

Just as I arrived at the pre-arranged Starbucks, my cell phone rang. It was the soon-to-be cover fish telling me he was going to be ten minutes late. He had a squeaky, effeminate quality to his voice, which I was hearing for the first time, and I was instantly turned off. I used my ten-minute reprieve to call Vicki and arrange an out. She was to send an urgent text in 45 minutes that she had just seen Travis headed toward the Cal Train station with a can of spray paint. Travis is no graffiti artist, but every parent lives in fear of the six-figure price tag that comes with defacing government property from the stories we read in the *San Jose Mercury News*. It worked like a charm. No sooner had we finished our first cup of coffee than the text came in. I turned my iPhone screen-first toward my date, and he said "You better go find him." I was released to go rescue the adolescent in my care, and my life savings, leaving no time to discuss a second date. It was a noble exodus.

Months later, standing at the Airport kiosk, I learned that *Squeaky Voice* was my missed opportunity for complete financial freedom – or could have been the *Sally Tomato* who would make me infamous, like Holly Golightly – but instead became another casualty of the catch and release strategy of a vegan fisherman. I scanned the article to learn that my abandoned catch had just become the Valley's newest overnight million-aire when his software company went public the week before. *What was it he said when I asked what he did for a living?* Software, I think. Just software. Every other fish in San Jose is in "software," and that usually means they are a programmer for one of the many software companies located here. He didn't say he had invented the software, and he failed to mention a looming IPO. He wasn't even driving a nice car, as I recall, but I'll bet he has a Bentley or a Ferrari (or perhaps both) now.

One of the first fish I hooked on-line was a man named Danny, and we went out a couple times. He had only been separated from his wife for a few weeks when we met, and it was clear by the second date that he was eager to be back on dry land. A lot of men don't like to be single, and Danny was one of them. They have no patience for the sport of fishing, and yearn to be caught and cared for by the first fisherman who pulls them out of the water. I told him on our second date that I was shell-shocked from my marriage ending, and not likely to walk down the aisle any time soon, if ever. He stopped calling. A week or so later, I noticed he had abandoned the pond, so I sent him a congratulatory email: "I see you have taken your profile down, and I assume it is because you have met someone special. I hope I'm right, really."

I meant it, too. Danny was sweet and deserved to be in a relationship. His matrimonial bliss had a sudden end when he discovered his wife was having an affair, so he hadn't taken the time to consider whether he was suited for the single life before packing a bag and moving to a hotel. Looking back, I recall him describing his wife then as "sexually charged," which I remember mostly because it contradicted the stories I heard from most newly divorced fish who typically tell of an ex who had lost interest in sex long before the marriage ended.

My congratulatory note sparked a response, which led to an e-conversation about monogamy, soul mates and sociology. Our chats continued over the next several months, and Danny became a friend. It seems that his life in the pond was short-lived, because he decided soon after our "break-up," as he called it, that he should forgive his wife and do what he could to fix his faltering marriage. Danny was no fish.

Danny's wife had a highly responsible job at a highly regarded technology company, and it was clear from his banter that she wore the pants in their family. Often our conversations veered toward his insecurity about making less money than her, which was unwarranted in my mind, because Danny had two successful patents to his name and I thought he was brilliant. Friends say I am easy to talk to, so it was not a complete surprise that I became Danny's close friend and confidant during that period of his life. I did not think of him as an ex. I hardly remembered after a while that I had encountered him first as a fish, since he was so grounded on dry land and I was thoroughly immersed in the sport by then.

On the first anniversary of my move to the fishbowl, I decided to have a party. I did not invite any fish, but I did invite Danny and suggested he bring his wife. My guest list consisted of clients and business associates, the Tail Club women, people from the club, chamber of commerce board colleagues, neighbors in the building, and the married people I spent more time with when I was half of a couple. It was a good crowd.

I love throwing parties, and it's the main reason I keep a large circle of friends handy. I hate the cooking, cleaning and shopping part, but I simply adore being in a room full of grateful people who all make a point of talking to me. The bonus is that I can drink like a fish and not worry about the drive home. I picked a night that Travis was away on college tours and both Linda and Vicki were in town, and made arrangements for both to sleep over. This would guarantee I wasn't the only drunk girl at my party, and would mean I had help cleaning the next day.

My younger sister and her husband are fabulous

cooks and neither of them drink. They offered to cater and bartend, as they always do, which is why my youngest sister, Jewel, will always be my favorite. My sister Dana came from Las Vegas, and she brought one of her boy toys as her date. I was a little embarrassed to introduce my flashy older sister and her 20-something friend to my business associates, but it turns out they were the least of my worries.

By 10:00 p.m., when Danny showed up and introduced me to his wife, I was pretty plowed. Mrs. Danny was one of the few party guests who was as tall as me in my 9-inch stripper shoes with goldfish in the plastic soles which – when added to my 5 foot, 5 inch frame – made me 6'2". Teetering on the shoes I had been given as a "bowl-warming" gift, I had to prop my drink on her shoulder when she came in for the hug. She was rambling on about how great it was to finally meet me and I thought for a minute that she had grabbed my butt. If she did, I convinced myself it was because I was about to fall over, and she was simply reaching for the most prominent part of my frame to offer stability.

Someone walked up to ask me a question, then Jewel needed a fresh platter to replace one that had fallen to the floor, and I excused myself to tend to hostess duties. Shortly after, I saw Danny and his wife talking to one of my clients, and then mingling with my lawyer, so they were proving to be the kind of guests that didn't need hand holding at a party, which is always a relief.

Sometime around midnight my stature was returned to its relatively diminutive size and someone had artfully placed one of my stripper shoes in the middle of a cheese platter. A bunch of grapes had been arranged where my foot had recently been, and cascaded beautifully around the plastic-encased goldfish, creating what I am pretty sure would constitute a health department violation. My other shoe was in someone's pants, the nine-inch heel protruding from his fly. Everyone was having fun, and most of those remaining appeared to be drunk. All the guests still present at that hour were downtowners who would be walking home, with the exception of Mr. and Mrs. Danny who had come from Palo Alto. Once I concluded I wouldn't need to arrange for any taxis, and saw that Danny was still sober, I made myself another drink. I could hear a loud, shrill laugh from across the room and surmised that Danny's wife – clearly the drinker in their family – was having a good time. I was still making my drink when she walked into the kitchen and grabbed my ass again. This time it was unmistakably intentional.

"You and I need to spend time together," she said, to which I enthusiastically agreed. I didn't want to have lunch or go shopping with Danny's wife, and I really didn't see her fitting in with the Tail Club, but my charm school training leads me to babble agreeably when I'm in a social setting. Vicki is always trying to reprogram my thinking in that regard. "That's the God damn charm school talking," she says whenever she sees me being nice to someone who doesn't deserve the courtesy. I was in one of those situations by letting Mrs. Danny's hand stay on my butt cheek, completely ignoring the instinct to send my knee into her groin. This was the first woman who had grabbed me like that, and *Sally Sears* did not prepare us for female aggression.

Danny came to my rescue, thankfully, and grabbed his wife's hand off my butt while he rolled his eyes in my direction. "I forgot to tell you that my wife likes her wine," he said in explanation, and that's when I noticed that she was even more hammered than I. They thanked me for the invitation, said they had a wonderful time, and Danny steered his wife toward the door. As soon as they were gone, Linda and Vicki converged on me with questions. "Who was that woman?" asked Linda, and before I could answer Vicki was saying, "She's a freak!"

It seems that Mrs. Danny had been indiscriminately grabbing butts throughout the evening and introducing herself to party guests as "the wife of my lover." *Excuse me? Danny and I were never lovers!* It gets worse. Linda said she heard her telling one of my clients that she and Danny were *swingers* and that I was joining them in a threesome. Danny's wife told my client that she wasn't sure if I was "into it" at first, but that I had agreed that night that it would be fun.

"Goddamn charm school!" shouted Vicki, and then she asked me to try to remember what I had agreed to. I thought about the conversation we had in the kitchen, when she had her hand on my ass. *She said something about getting together... just the two of us, or maybe with Danny... but I thought she was talking about having lunch!*

Crap, crap, crap. This was a disaster! Who did she

talk to? How much damage control was needed? What if my company loses a client or two because they think one of the principals is a sex fiend? My mind was racing with the potential fallout from this black smear on my reputation. *My business partners were going to kill me... this would factor against me in my divorce settlement... I may be asked to resign my seat on the chamber board... Child Protective Services would be coming for Travis!*

The next morning Vicki, Linda and I continued our discussion about events of the evening, sober over breakfast, and they convinced me my hysteria was unwarranted. Linda noted that Mrs. Danny was too drunk to be taken seriously by anyone who she may have talked to, and Vicki thought it unlikely that anyone would cancel a contract with my agency over something heard at a party. Good girlfriends will be the first to tell you when you've screwed up, and the last remaining to help clean up the mess after the damage is done. I was glad I did not have to suffer this morning after alone.

Danny called nonchalantly the next day to thank me again for the party, and no mention was made of his spouse's behavior. "I'm glad you finally got to meet my wife," he said, and I responded with the usual "it was my pleasure" crap that has been tattooed on my tongue since charm school. I didn't end our friendship at that moment, although I should have, but I removed Danny from my call list, and our conversations became less frequent and the relationship faded over time.

Except for some unusual looks I got over the next few days from people who had swam in the fish bowl that night, which I may have imagined, there was no fall-out from the party that impacted my livelihood, my parental status, or my standing in the community. I patted myself on the back for the decision to not invite any fish to my party, and imagined how much worse it might have been if my house had been filled with Bobs and Mikes and men with squeaky voices who drove very rare Harleys, in addition to a bisexual female predator.

Danny's wife had more physical contact with me that night than most of my dates do, for the amount of time she held my butt cheek in the palm of her hand. So, by the Tail Club's definition of what constitutes an "ex," Danny's wife is one of the fish from my past. When I consider that she is tall, attractive, masculine, and successful, I would have considered her to be a great catch, if only she was single. I guess a penis would help too, but maybe I'm being too picky.

27
Five Dollar Blowjobs

There was a woman I used to see when I lived in New York. She was always in the vicinity of Madison Square Garden, and she would walk up to men and say, "Blowjob, five dollars." She had her hair pulled back in a high ponytail, which made sense in her line of work, as it provided customers with a handle and it kept her hair out of her mouth.

My ex-husband used to make a comment every time I wore my hair in a high ponytail. "Goin' to work today?" he would say, to which I would respond, "You got five dollars, mister?"

So for years when I have found myself in a financial bind or if business is down at the agency, I have taken strange comfort from knowing I have never had to sell five-dollar blowjobs to make the mortgage payment.

Since I have been single, however, I realize how much I rely on men to make ends meet, and sometimes fear I have become more like the pony-tailed woman at Madison Square Garden than ever before in my adult life. The funny thing about men is this: they love to give women money, and most of the time they don't expect anything in return. Ponytail lady could have made as much money with the line "You're handsome, can I have five dollars?" and saved a lot of strain on her jaw muscles in the process.

I made the mistake once of telling a fish I was too broke to do any traveling, and he gave me $500. I assumed, of course, he was expecting a hundred blowjobs in return, and would not accept the money. He said he wanted me to have the money, because it was such a shame that I couldn't travel.

When it happened the second time, after another innocent remark about not having the money to buy a new car, I arrived at this theory: you can angst out loud to other women about the things you can't afford, but men will see it as a call to action. It's hard not to love men for possessing this basic need to provide, and I imagine the difficult adjustment alpha male providers have to make when they no longer have wives and families to support. Tempting as it was to accept the cash – from men who really wanted to give me money – this constitutes "powder room change" no matter how you look at it, and this is where the parallels between Holly Golightly and me end.

I joke with my girlfriends about dating to eat, as I have been known to make fish dates for dinner on nights when I have nothing to eat in my house. I call that "blowjob money," even though I don't actually have to give anyone a blowjob, and seldom go home with five dollars in my pocket. In my mind, it's the same principle.

I feel guilty about being plied with fine food and

expensive drinks, particularly when I'm not terribly interested in the man, but it's important to establish on the coffee date that they have the money to some day buy me dinner. My coffee date with a fish named James started with the telling of his recently failed marriage. He described the divorce proceedings as "the War of the Roses," and I pictured a house being dismantled piece by piece while two lawyers split the retirement account. I wasn't surprised, therefore, when the check came and James said my tall latte' had cost $4.25, and with tip I owed him $5. I gave him a five-dollar bill, with no expectation of a blowjob, and then I released him.

Molly said she has a rule about who pays. "On date two or three, I might offer to pick up the tab, or split it in two, but there won't be a second date if the hierarchy of who pays is not established up front," she said.

I found that interesting coming from Molly, since she got a very healthy settlement from her ex, and is perhaps the highest paid executive assistant in the Valley. Of all my single female friends, Molly is in the best position to support a boy toy, so I wouldn't think economics would be as important to her. It just goes to show that it's not really about the money. Women want to know whether the fish can afford to be on the date, and whether he picks up the check is the quickest way to make that determination.

The five dollar blowjob lady and the men who take her up on her offer are, in my mind, exhibiting the purest form of preliminary relationship behavior. The rest of us make complicated rules about whom we will sleep with, and how much they need to spend before they are deserving of our favors; and men expect to receive return on their investment, and have their own rules about how much cash they will fork-out before they cut bait. It's a business transaction, with lower stakes.

The stakes can be higher than a few dinners or a five-dollar bill too. Molly was dating the member of a very exclusive country club for about a year. When he added her to his membership – which meant she could use the club facilities whenever she wanted with or without the boyfriend present – it became a huge issue when the relationship went sour. We were all growing accustomed to Friday golf and Sunday Brunch at the Club, and Molly had established a beachhead there. The staff knew her name; and everyone at the club knew what she liked for lunch, her favorite drink, her friends' names, and they kept track of her golf scores. The relationship hung on by a thread about six months longer than it should have. Molly was done with the man, but could not fathom the thought of losing the club. None of us could, really.

I have heard that call girls get between $2,000 and $5,000 for an evening, and wonder if there is also expectation the man will pay for everything during the "date" as well. In business, gender roles are cast aside and the client (male or female) would not be expected to pick up the check for lunch. If business rules apply in the sex-for-hire game, does the cost of her meal and the drinks she consumes get deducted from the final bill? I am not sure how to find this out, but it's interesting to think that regular women are significantly less expensive than professionals. The fact that call girls and prostitutes exist, and the industry thrives in every economy, just goes to show that many men – despite their competitive nature – would rather spend big bucks for a sure thing than play in a fishing tournament for less cash.

When I think about it, even my preparation for a fish date is largely about profit and loss. I dress better if I think the date has the money to take me some place nice, and I spend more time on hair and makeup too, because I want him to see me as a worthwhile investment. I have never worn my hair in a high ponytail on a date, and the thought of five dollar blowjob lady may have subconsciously guided me to cut my hair shorter when I became single.

While I draw the line at cash gifts, semi-professional, competitive fishing has been a lucrative venture. After I had been in the pond for seven or eight months, I made a list of all the gifts and favors I had received from fish, and realized I had made a decent profit for the small investment I made in three lucky blouses and a handful of minnow dates I paid for.

All-in-all, I went on 50 or so fish dates and received:

- 9 complimentary massages (estimated value $675)
- 15 free meals (estimated value $750)
- 4 dozen roses (estimated value $144)
- free legal advice (estimated value $700)
- a free chiropractic adjustment (estimated value $95)

- 36 grande lattes (estimated value $117)
- Amazon Kindle (estimated value $300)
- 100 or more vodka tonics with a splash o'cran (estimated value $1,000)
- a car battery (estimated value $95)
- two bottles of Ketel One (estimated value $60)
- a new convertible top on my BMW (estimated value $2,600)
- a new clutch installed in my BMW (estimated value $1,200)
- 100 shares of pre-IPO stock in a Silicon Valley company (cannot disclose value)

and:

- 5 Harley rides (priceless)
- 12 trips in really cool cars (priceless)
- a 175 mph ride in a race car (really priceless)
- an upside-down ride in a decommissioned Navy jet (beyond priceless)

Any capitalist could see that fishing is way better economics than "getting out there" in bars with girlfriends. I don't have to sell blowjobs, seldom pay for my own drink, and I meet a lot of nice fish.

The second time I turned down the offer of cash from a fish, he asked if I would have accepted jewelry instead. I waffled in my answer because the truth is, I would have. For some reason, material goods and/or an expensive dinner were not the same as cash to me, but in his mind there was no difference. "Either way, I am going to spend money on you, and it seems silly to buy someone jewelry when they are driving a 15 year-old car."

My practical mind couldn't argue with his logic, but I was pretty happy with my old BMW, and never satisfied with the contents of my jewelry box. My capitalistic mind once again wandered off to dollars and cents and profit and loss, and for a moment I lost sight of the discussion I was having with a fish about dating ethics. Then I remembered I was an independent who didn't like to be indebted to anyone, and realized that I could still afford to buy myself jewelry every now and then, and remembered that I don't ask for powder room change or sell five dollar blowjobs.

I reluctantly released the fish that wanted to give me cash instead of jewelry, and maintained righteous indignation about his offer until the day the clutch went out in my old BMW. Luckily, his number was still in my phone.

28
Washed Up

The day I stopped being Holly Golightly was my 51st birthday, but it took about a week to make the realization. I was lavishing in birthday celebrations for a few days, and had neglected my livewell. By the time I signed on to *Plenty of Fish* after a short hiatus, there were plenty of fish awaiting my perusal, as is usually the case when I stay off the pond for a few days. I started my standard review, and picked a few fish to make a date with, since I had the next two nights free for the first time in a long while.

The first fish I looked at was a 48 year-old engineer who got the reference to Holly Golightly in my profile, and had read everything written by Truman Capote. Yes, he will do. I wrote him a quick, pithy email about my favorite Capote stories; asked which screen version of *In Cold Blood* he had liked the best; and mentioned I was free that night if he was.

The reply was too quick to be human: *You are over the minimum age to contact this fish.*

The dreaded blocking message. I had seen it only once before, when I tried to forward a fish to Mike for his review by using his username, unaware that he had blocked anyone over the age of 45 from contacting him.

Mike was an ageist, and would often say things to me that were offensive, but I learned not to let it get to me. One morning when we were still friends, he came in to tell me about a date he went on with a woman he called "well preserved" for 42. Ouch. If 42 year-olds need "preserving," then all the Botox in the world couldn't help 50 year-olds like me, I thought. Well, that's Mike, I told myself, and thanked God and *Plenty of Fish* that he was not in the majority as fish go. I had my minnows to give me comfort, after all, because fish like Mike were the reason I did not block teenage boys from contacting me.

The blocking mechanism of *Plenty of Fish* is used primarily by men of a certain age who find women of that same age to be offensive. We women of that certain age are completely repulsive to these men, and the mere thought of us trying to make contact will send them running to the men's room to lose their lunch. Once you have set blockers in place, anyone who attempts to contact you that is over the pre-set age limit will get the message. It doesn't happen very often, though, because with blockers in place, everyone who is over your pre-set limit is ejected from your pond. They don't exist for you, and you don't exist for them. So the only way the blocking message is brought into play is when you try to respond to a message right after your birthday, or when you try to contact someone, like I did with Mike, who would be invisible to you if you didn't know his username.

This is mood-crushing information I have been presented with: there are fish who find me so repulsive they have taken steps to keep my rusty, corroded hook out of their face. Every birthday since the 40th has been hard to take, but this one – thanks to the evildoers in the *Plenty of Fish* I.T. department – will go down as the birthday that transformed the chubby teenager I see in the mirror every day to a skinny, stooped, grey-haired Granny Clampett overnight. My Capote-loving engineer was interested in me on Tuesday, but got a restraining order against me on Friday of the same week.

Fish message after fish message came back with the blocking dispatch, until my livewell was empty. My fishing days were over, or my catching days to be more accurate.

Then I remembered *OKCupid*, another dating site my sister Dana had told me about. Do they have blocking ability? No, they do not. And matches are sent to me for review, instead of making me fish the whole pond. *Quiver Matches* as they call them are specially selected because of common answers to questions about values, lifestyle and politics. So everyone sent for my consideration has already been pre-screened as a person who is ideologically suited for me. Unfortunately, a lot of them are not so attractive to me, but no matter.

After a couple days on *OKCupid*, I got an email from one of the fish that had blocked me on *Plenty of Fish*, and totally ruined my birthday. "Hey, you didn't respond to me on POF, so I thought I would try you here," *Bikerdude* wrote. I responded by explaining that I was too old for him, noting in his preferences he stated a desire to date no one older than 50.

Holly Golightly would be 72 years old today, and I choose to believe she still looks good in a little black dress. I have many more years of fishing ahead of me, and neither Holly nor I would be interested in a man of any age with the username of "Bikerdude" anyway. So when he emailed me again with something he intended as a compliment, it made me mad as hell instead. "Wow, you're 51? You only look 35, so I would be happy to meet you."

The fact that this 54 year-old fish was ONLY willing to date someone three years YOUNGER than him if she looked considerably younger than him was infuriating to me in light of the numerous blocking messages I had just received from fish around my same age. I checked out Bikerdude's full profile and saw he had set his age requirements all the way down to 25, but limited the top end to 50. He was willing to date children, because he could have easily had a daughter who was 25 or even 35, but he was not willing to date women his own age.

I almost broke my keyboard from pounding out my response. *I don't date pedophiles* was all I wrote. Then, still steaming, I sent him a second email detailing the many ways in which I found him to be unattractive and added that he appeared to look every bit his age.

Age is relative. I may look 35 years old to Biker-dude, but let's see if he's impressed to know I can act like a 15-year-old under the right influence.

29
The Piss Boy: a Love Story

Several years before I started talking in fishing metaphors, I used dog metaphors a lot. Married life could best be described as if I was living life in a collar and sometimes a choke chain. Girl's Weekend was going "off-leash." Going out dancing was a romp in the "dog park." And territorial husbands or boyfriends were described as "markers." When my husband was in one of his rare possessive moods, I would ask the Tail Club members if I smelled like urine.

So even though Todd did a thorough job of marking me even before I was single, it is not how he came to be known by everyone as The Piss Boy.

I guess you could say I met Todd on a bet.

All of the women who spend time with Molly at her country club play a game called "points." In golf, points are given for the obvious things like longest drive, and less obvious accomplishments like having the most color-coordinated golf ensemble. Off the course, points are issued for things you can get a man to do. If we're at a bar, for example, the first woman to get a man to buy all of us a round of drinks gets 50 points.

Ten points for every drink you fail to pay for yourself after that, and bonus points if you can get a man to drive us home after we've had a particularly successful session of racking up points.

Molly has a second home in La Quinta, near Palm Springs, and she, Vicki and I went there for a weekend, after her seasonal renters had left, to make repairs and check on the house. The damage we found upon arrival was considerably more extensive than she had imagined, and we realized this was more than just a paint and spackle job, which we thought we could handle.

Vicki put 200 points at stake if I could find a man to stay with us at the house for the remainder of the weekend to make necessary repairs. Bonus points if I could get him to be our complete slave, which meant applying suntan lotion to our backs when we were poolside, and delivering cocktails and snacks to us in the hot tub. And he would receive nothing in return, except the privilege of being in our company. This, we determined, would be the ultimate points challenge any of us had ever attempted.

We knew just where to find a thrall in the desert: a piano bar in Indian Wells called *The Nest*. Todd was there with a large group of men who were all on a guy's trip away from their wives and families. We bee-lined for the only remaining table at the same time as Todd's group, and agreed the table was large enough to share. After introductions were made, I identified Todd as the mark because he was newly divorced, recently unemployed, and the father of a teenager away at boarding school. He was the only man in the group who seemed to have no one at home who would be missing him and no job to get back to. Extra bonus points: he was cute.

I thought I worked the whole scheme pretty well. First, we let the group buy us drinks, then I asked Todd if he could drive us home in our car, assuring him we would put him in a taxi back to his hotel as soon as we got there. Once he had driven us the half hour to La Quinta, we suggested he come in for a nightcap, and that's where we laid out the proposition. It started with me breaking the news that we were not intending to put him in a taxi home, and that he was not going to make his morning flight. He reacted with unexpected delight.

"So what you're looking for is a piss boy," he said after he heard our pitch. The Piss Boy was a character from the Mel Brooks movie *History of the World, Part Two*, in which a character called The Piss Boy followed the king and his court around with a piss bucket, and was at their service 24/7. "Yes," said Molly. "Except for the piss bucket, that is exactly what we want from you."

Now, if three men lured me to a remote desert home and then told me I was their captive slave, I would cry and beg for my life. Todd just smiled and started making cell phone calls – first to the guys back at *The Nest*, then to his dog-sitter at home in Denver, and finally to United Airlines to push his departure back two days. He excitedly asked for paper and a pen and started to make a list of the tools he would need to procure the next day, but only after he freshened our cocktails and set out a plate of crackers with goat cheese and sun-dried tomatoes.

The next day he gave us all foot massages before he drove us to the nail salon, and lunch was served poolside when we returned. While we were being pampered, he had fixed the sliding glass door squeak; unclogged the sink in the wet bar; repaired a broken chair in the kitchen; and replaced all the burned out light bulbs in the house. All that was left for him to do was patch and paint, and address my lower back issue. We could not have chosen a better piss boy.

The weekend with Todd the piss boy was several months before I found myself suddenly single, but he kept in touch. He had family in San Jose, and came to visit fairly often. Every time he was in town he would call to ask if we needed any piss boy services. We never did, but he came to The Grill on the Alley to meet us for a drink on one such visit, and it was good to see him. The next time he was in San Jose for a family event, happened to be the weekend my husband moved out.

As could be expected, the piss boy jumped in to service. Todd called to say he was in town with nothing to do. I told him I was busy watching my husband pack, and then thought better. "Pick me up in 10 minutes," I said, "because we're going out on a date."

So Todd was my *actual* first date, even before my first attempt at Internet dating. It turns out he is more insightful than I thought, for a piss boy that is. He confessed to keeping in touch all these months on the chance that I would become single eventually. He said he sensed my marriage wasn't on strong footing when he saw me on the phone with my husband in La Quinta. I didn't even know I was on the verge of being dumped at that time, but he noted how my mood soured and my brow furrowed when I saw my life-partner's name on my phone. "That told me I should keep in touch," he confessed, and Vicki encouraged him in that regard too as she already saw the signs that my marriage was crumbling.

Looking back at how I met Todd, I realize how much I took men for granted when I was married, and I'm starting to face up to the reality that I really was a very bad wife. My third marriage was on shaky ground, but I was away on one of many weekends with girl-friends, cringing when I saw my husband's name on my phone, because it meant he was going to take me away from my cocktail or my back rub with talk of responsi-bilities at home or at the office. Our marriage at that point was less about shared passions, of which there were few by then, and more about shared responsibil-ities, for which I also have to take some ownership. And even though Todd gave himself the moniker, I still sometimes shudder to think of the weekend in which we made him our slave, and marvel that his sense of humor on the subject has remained in tact.

Over the next year-and-a-half, the long-distance relationship with Todd continued.

I could count on him to be in San Jose at least one weekend out of every month, and sometimes – when piss boy services are needed – he would stay for a whole week; like when I moved into the fishbowl, or when Vicki moved into a new condo, and we both needed window coverings installed, rooms painted and wired for light fixtures, new appliances... the stuff people from Venus can't do. And when I really need an escort to an event not befitting a fish, such as Jeremy and Megan's wedding, Todd will make a special trip.

Todd comes to see me mostly, but I get to Denver at least two or three times a year, mostly during the ski season. Linda met a man from Atlanta on *Plenty of Fish*, and she's been traveling back and forth for the last month or so to see him. My sister Dana is considering a move to Pennsylvania for a fish she has been in a long-distance relationship with for more than a year. Between the two of them and Vicki, with her frequent trips back to Chicago, scheduling girlfriend trips to La Quinta or to Salem for the Witchcraft Festival has become increasingly difficult. We are all using our frequent flyer points on fish dates afar, which we have dubbed "fly fishing," because it seems the most interesting fish are the "elsewhere men" you have to get on an airplane to date.

Todd is steadfast in his quest to never remarry, so this is the perfect relationship for both of us. "We are always too happy to see each other to get into a fight," he pointed out one day when he was expounding the many, many benefits of our part-time, long-distance, non-committed relationship, and I had to agree.

I see Todd's visits as a "break" from being single. We act like a married couple when he's here. He makes home and auto repairs during the day, we have dinner together at night, and then we just stay home and watch TV, which I have never once done by myself since I have been single. After he leaves I feel a void for a day or so, and it sometimes makes me miss having a husband. More often, though, I am glad to get back to my real life of fishing, and having cocktails with friends, and eating in restaurants, and going to movies instead of watching TV.

Todd and I went to great lengths for a good year to avoid words like "boyfriend" and "girlfriend," and never, ever, ever used the "L" word by mutual agreement. This relationship would be light, fun, non-committed, drama-free, and part-time, so we said. He was the first to blurt out "I love you" once on the phone when he was obviously drunk. I made him take it back, and he apologized the next day. Drunk talk or not, it broke a barrier, and we both started to let our guard down in that regard. So yes, I love Todd, but it doesn't change anything.

My relationship with Todd continues, and I haven't called him *the piss boy* in a long while. Now he's the *Denver boyfriend*, or just *Denver* to a lot of people. We're both in the pond, and he has adopted the poly philosophy of relationships like me. He says he doesn't date much, and insists he's okay with me dating other men as long as I don't give him details. He says our relationship could go on indefinitely as it is, but I once overheard him telling a friend he thought our relationship would last until I met someone who was richer and better looking than him. Great minds think alike, I guess, because that is how I believe our relationship will end too, but in my version it is he who meets someone better suited to be his next wife.

Our two-year anniversary is coming up in a few

months, and we're planning to meet in Las Vegas to celebrate. It will be our first time together in neutral territory – where there will be nothing for him to fix or to maintain, there will be no kitchen in which to prepare meals, and I can't imagine we will watch any television. It will be interesting to be on a real date with Todd, in a city where playing house is frowned upon. Will the relationship survive Vegas? We shall see.

30
Wine Not Whine

Drinking red wine gives me a headache of the worst kind that never goes away with aspirin or time, and it only takes a glass or two to get me drunk in a bad way –slurring my words, falling down, and acting kind of mean. It turns out I am allergic to tannins.

Except for the final result, I like everything about wine, though. I adore wine glasses, wine labels and wine accessories; especially the artisan-created wines-stoppers of which I have started to collect, and I'm okay with a glass or two of Chardonnay, for some reason. I love wine country scenery – rows of perfectly mani-cured vines meandering over oak-studded, rolling hills – and I love the sights and smells of a winery, even though my eyes water when I'm in one. There is almost always a cute little tasting room; sometimes the décor is contemporary, sometimes Italian, sometimes French Provincial – but always quaint and tastefully appointed – with a gift shop and often a small gallery exhibiting painted landscapes of wine country. When the tannins become overwhelming, I step outside to play with a winery dog or two, because winemaking seems to go hand-in-hand with big, friendly hounds. I like to take pictures of grapes on the vine in their varicolored clusters; plump, juicy black balls with some purple and pink, and a few little green dots representing grapes that never came to fruition. One of those grape bunch pictures is the screen-saver on my laptop.

I looked forward to the day I would scrub my feet and step into a barrel full of freshly picked fruit and then dance lightly in a small circle to feel grapes squishing under my feet and slipping between my toes to be caught on the next pass. That was the image that came to mind six years ago when I agreed to let my husband plant 100 Syrah vines in the backyard of our lakehouse on the outskirts of Paso Robles, which is central California's burgeoning new wine country. The vines will be pretty, I thought, and I could advertise the back-facing bedrooms with no view of the lake as having a "vineyard view" when I put the house on the rental market. Everyone wins.

My husband had a passion for wine. He could taste the difference between a great wine and a pedestrian wine, and made a rather sizable investment in bottles from the former category, and then an even greater investment in building a wine cave to store his collection at optimal temperature until they were ready for consumption. I still call him my soon-to-be-ex-husband, because we're not divorced yet, but he refers to me as his "partner" or his "associate" to differentiate me from his girlfriend and constant companion, who now works with us at the Agency and has moved in to his condo.

Our new "general manager" is my partner's new passion, and I have found the arrangement to be less awkward than one might think. She has taken over the long vacant position that was Diane's job before she died, and it's good to have someone in that role.

My husband's passions changed often during our marriage, and every new venture was approached with one hundred percent of his time and enthusiasm. Seeing him dote on the new girlfriend reminds me of a day when he was that attentive to me. In the beginning of our marriage his first passion was starting the business, which is a passion we both embraced wholeheartedly. Then it was an interest in restoring a classic car; then he started collecting old radios; then it was the wine cave and the vineyard; and the final iteration of his mid-life crisis was the formation of the classic rock cover band, which became the breaking point in our relationship because I really don't like the Rolling Stones.

His changing passions succeeded in dampening mine, and I checked out of the extra-curricular part of our marriage somewhere in the vineyard I believe. When he left he took his guitar, two drum kits and a large arsenal of sound equipment, but left the never-touched classic car, the cellar full of expensive wine, and the lakehouse and vineyard in Paso Robles in my passionless hands.

Maintaining the lakehouse and managing it as a rental property is a big job, as it turns out, and I am forever grateful to have so many friends, an occasional fish, and a wonderfully supportive family to help me in that regard. My cocky optimism in the early days of being single was unwarranted, it seems. "I can do this," was replaced with "please can you help me?" as my go-to phrase, when I came to realize that keeping the lakehouse until the real estate market improved was a huge responsibility.

The old car my husband purchased with the intent of restoring was still in the lakehouse garage, covered with a canvas tarp. It was a 1964 Dodge Dart convertible – the 25th Anniversary edition – with chrome inlay on the steering wheel column proclaiming it to be a limited edition V-8 with four on the floor. Todd discovered the car one day when he was helping me make repairs at the lakehouse, and said he could help me to restore it. That is, if I wanted to adopt one of my soon-to-be-ex-husbands abandoned passions, and for whatever reason I said that I did. I needed to have something to do at the lakehouse that could be finished some day – something that would provide me with a sense of accomplishment, beyond simply knowing the house would stand for another month.

Todd's passion for cars has not waned over time, and I didn't know until I met him how hungry I was for something to be passionate about. We had little in common at first, except that we were both unintentionally single, and we share a common allergy to tannins. Now we have classic cars in common, which started with restoring the Dart, a project that was completed in just three dedicated weekends of hard work.

Todd picked up where my dad left off (about the

time I hit puberty) by reminding me to appreciate the inner-workings of an old engine, and showed me how new chrome can make a 50-year-old car look brand new. Even mundane trips to Costco or to pick up a pizza are special occasions when you do it in a shiny old convertible that looks like it just rolled off the showroom floor. People point and wave, and I can't resist taking children for rides around the parking lot when they ask. It's a nice way to spend a day.

Making wine was not an attempt to steal another of my soon-to-ex-husband's abandoned passions. It was a spontaneous decision that started with a fateful moment. I was at the lakehouse for a week with my family – two sisters, one brother-in-law, three nephews, two nieces, and two parents – when I saw that birds were in the process of ravaging the vineyard. Remembering that a winemaker once told me the best way to know when your grapes are ready without a sugar-tester was to watch the birds. "They want them when you want them," he had said.

Everything just seemed right. The grapes were ready, and I had a crew for an entire week. My field labor consisted of five teenagers who couldn't drink wine by law, a sister and a father who share my intolerance for tannins, another sister and brother in-law who don't drink at all, and a mother who is diabetic. So there was not one member of my winemaking crew who would be able to enjoy the fruits of our labor. I sent everyone up to the vineyard with a basket, a cooler or a paper bag – whatever I could find for this impromptu harvest, assuming it would take just a few minutes to pick all the grapes with such a large crew. It ended up taking four days to clear 90 or so vines, but we never got to the last row.

I had this picture in my mind of walking through a row of vines and picking them clean in minutes. Half my crew (including myself) could not stand in the vineyard for more than a few minutes before our eyes were watering so bad we couldn't see the grapes anymore. And it took standing at one vine for about a half hour to pick all its fruit. It seems the best clusters were close to the trunk, and usually surrounded by a tangle of leaves, so it took some pruning to get at them. And there were so many. Fifty or so grape bunches on every vine. A half hour at each vine multiplied by 100 vines is 50 hours – simple math even I can do. The bored teenagers were only good for an hour a day, and half my adult pickers could only work in half-hour increments with a one-hour break in-between, and then there was some unidentifiable insect that was biting us all and leaving ugly, itchy welts. It seemed to take forever to get the grapes into my stomping tub.

Still my passion for making wine grew as the harvest continued. I was getting excited as I saw the grapes pile up into a respectable quantity, but I couldn't stand near the tub for too long as the increasing concentration of tannins was making it hard to breath. I was designing a wine label in my head and fantasizing about turning the wine cave into a tasting room, and my sister's pug Rachel into a winery dog. "Red Passion" would be my label, and *I* would be the winemaker.

After the third picking day we discovered that Rachel had been eating our grapes and had a nasty intestinal infection, which grew worse every hour. By day four she was continuously emitting blackish-colored, ink-like fluid from her backside, and I lost one of my pickers to get her to a veterinary hospital 40 miles away and lost another picker to steam cleaning the carpets. Clearly Rachel did not have the constitution to be a winery dog.

On the fifth day the harvest was as done as it could be, because everyone on my picking crew was too covered with insect bites to continue. It was time for the crush. I scrubbed my feet in the bathtub, and then walked to the vat of grapes wearing an abandoned pair of my soon-to-be-ex-husband's socks. I peeled them off at the edge of the grape vat and stepped in. Crushing grapes with my bare feet felt exactly like I imagined it would, except that in my fantasy crush I did not have an allergic reaction that made my eyes swell shut by the time the fruit took liquid form.

I found a small winery that would take my vat of squished grapes and age them in an oak barrel at the appropriate temperature for the appropriate amount of time, so in several months I will have wine. My passion will be in every bottle and it shows in the label I've already designed, and the packaging I've already developed, and the little card I've already written explaining that each bottle contains my sweat and my tears and hopefully nothing else besides crushed Syrah grapes and a little yeast. I will never drink any of the wine I made, but I don't need to. Making it fulfilled all the passion for wine I have.

It turns out that passion comes from within; it's not sparked by a shiny chrome bumper, a sip of great wine, or a kiss from an interesting admirer. When I was ready to embrace life with all my energy and enthusiasm, the passion followed. I understand now why people develop a passion for collecting Pez dispensers or old fishing lures. I think I could find passion in collecting and restoring staplers and three-hole punches if I learned a little about their history and figured out what it took to make them shiny again. I was beyond the buried rage of my husband's mutiny, and had gotten past the increasingly felt burden of contrasting his fleeting passions with a grounded sense of hyper-responsibility. I love taking care of the lakehouse, the vineyard, and the car now. You could say they are my passion.

31
Happily Ever After

Holly Golightly thought nothing bad could ever happen at Tiffany's, and I believe that nothing life-changing can ever happen at home. Every day when I leave my fishbowl I wonder if this is a day that might send me in another direction, because I never know when moments of fate are going to present themselves.

The moment my marriage ended and my new journey began was an ordinary Wednesday just over two years ago. My husband and I were meeting my parents and Travis for dinner at a favorite downtown restaurant. My parents were coming from their home in the suburbs, Travis was coming from school, I was coming straight from a meeting, and my husband was coming from the office. I arrived before the others, because my meeting had ended early, so I went straight to the bar thinking I would have time for a cocktail before the family arrived. It wasn't yet five o'clock.

Two very attractive women about my age were sitting backwards at the bar, which is something one does when wishing to appear easy to approach. There was no one else in the room at this early hour, so their pose struck me as odd. It also seemed out of place that these two women were dressed in Saturday night attire and "special occasion" make-up (as I called it in my charm school essay), when this was a Wednesday and it was still too early for even the happy hour crowd. The women greeted me with something friendly like "If you're alone, you can join us," to which I said I was waiting for my family, and then ordered a drink and excused myself to the restroom.

I didn't need to go, but something about these overly friendly women made me want to get away from them. I was overtaken by sudden panic and found myself hyper-ventilating in the restroom mirror. Aloud, between breaths, I said - "Please God – save my – marriage – so I – don't have – to be like – those women."

Those women were "out there" at the bar waiting for the happy hour crowd to roll in so they could meet men. They were fishing at 50, and the sight of them had a visceral effect on my central nervous system. I stayed in the restroom for as long as it took to contain myself, which was considerably longer than the time required for your average pee. When I came back to the bar my husband was in an animated conversation with the women, which seemed loud for an early hour before anyone could be even a little intoxicated. My emergence from the restroom was perfectly timed with my parents and Travis' arrival, so my slow walk back to the bar area to get my drink was aborted and we went directly to the dining room. Further conversation with the friendly women was averted.

My husband made a few trips back to the bar

during dinner: once to settle the check for our cock-tails, and again to talk to the manager about the potential of hiring his band. Both times he stopped for a short chat with the women who were still seated approachably backwards at the bar. On his second trip I saw the prettier of the two write something on a napkin, and I saw him put the napkin in his pocket. My mother witnessed it too, because she patted my hand under the table.

My husband started acting differently the next day, and the affair was confirmed with a phone call from a woman I know who saw them together only two weeks later.

"Your husband is having an affair," said the caller, to which I simply said, "I know."

I did know, but I didn't know. I knew something had changed in my marriage, and that my husband had completed his check-out. I knew that a fateful event had taken place on that Wednesday night, but I misin-terpreted the event as a wake-up call that I needed to save my marriage and not as a sign it was over. My husband collected telephone numbers from women all the time, after all, and always had a lot of female friends. I knew the kind of man I had married – a hope-less flirt and a sportfisherman who loves to be in the company of women. It did not occur to me then my visceral reaction to these attractive, approachable contemporaries was a subconscious realization that I was laying eyes on the woman who wanted my life.

Despite what I first sensed and soon confirmed, I did nothing to save my marriage after that night, except perhaps think about it a little more than usual, and I guess I did go buy that eyelash-growing tonic.

The lingering reaction I had to the sight of those women in the bar that Wednesday night is this: I am still uncomfortable "getting out there" to meet men, so I contain my fishing to the Internet, and sit forward at a bar because I am never in a bar for the specific purpose of meeting men. Except for that first night that Vicki and I went to *Steamers* and found we were in a sea of over-dressed single women, and despite my feeling that alcohol is a love potion, I have not once gone fishing for men in a bar. I go to bars with friends to socialize with the people I am with, and on occasion have happened upon a fish or two. I met Todd in a bar, after all, and the Prince who bit me. Johnny too.

Johnny is a friend who gave me perhaps the best, and surely the most contrary, advice of any I heard just a few weeks into my new life as a single person. He was a man about ten years older than me who was sitting alone at *The Grill*, eavesdropping on my conversation with Linda about the recent end to my marriage. I think we were planning our trip to the northeast then. When Linda went to the ladies room, Johnny slid over to the barstool next to mine and spoke to me. "Honey, give yourself a year or two to get used to the idea of being single, and when you do – he looked around to make sure no one was listening, as if he was about to give me the secret password to happiness – "you are going to find it is a wonderful way to live."

Johnny went on to tell me he had been happily divorced for 23 years and had more friends, more hobbies and more interests than he ever had when he was married. He told me to establish a great life for myself, a life that doesn't depend on someone else to be complete. "Once you do," he said, "then everyone you meet after that has to live up to some very high standards."

I have applied that principle over and over again on dates, and it's probably the reason most of my fish are released. I ask myself: is this person so wonderful to be around that I would compromise this great life I have to be with them? The more whole my personage becomes, the more often the answer to that question is NO.

I look at the high divorce rate in this country, and the even higher divorce rate for second marriages, and I can't help but wonder if everyone would be happier in their marriages if they took more time establishing themselves as a single entity first. I feel sorry for people who replace one spouse with another as soon as the ink is dry on their divorce papers, because they have not taken the time to learn the power of being a whole, single person instead of half of a whole couple. And some people never achieve more than being a quarter of a whole couple, or half of a half couple, but I probably shouldn't try to make points with fractions, since I'm not good at math.

Johnny was about to be married again to a woman he had been dating for the last five years. He got teary-eyed when he told Linda and me how wonderful she was, and said he woke up in her bed one morning and realized – for the first time in 20 years – that he didn't want to leave.

That's what I want. Not the sentimental man who tears up when he talks about me (I would probably hate that,) I mean the wonderful life that doesn't depend on another person to be complete.

Despite my fear-induced panic attack in the restroom two years ago, I have found that I am fairly content being single. I enjoy going out on dates, especially first dates when I am not disappointed, and I'm not sure anymore if I am looking for Mister Right or Mister Right Now. I like getting to know new people, and I am grateful to have so many old and new friends in the pond and on dry land to spend time with. The single life is by no means a lonely life; so don't believe what you see in chick flicks starring Diane Keaton.

A single person cannot have too many friends in my opinion. It takes a village of Johnnys, Todds, Teds, Bobs, and Mikes and an entire Tail Club of women to keep one human being happy, healthy and with all the benefits of a family. I learn something from everyone I know, and I have learned something from every date too. I am better able to articulate what I am looking for after dating a lot of men who didn't fit the bill; and I am more grounded in reality for the men who rejected me, or didn't want a second date.

The pond is a friendly place, between the women who want to share fishing stories when they meet the end of another line in the water, to the fish dates that were all talk and no chemistry, yet the conversations continue. It's okay now when fish only nibble, because sometimes a prince will bite.

If my story resolves with a chick-flick ending I will

meet a man and presumably live happily every after, right? Ever-after is as fuzzy to me as math, but to make another lame attempt at math I would say I am two times happier now than I was when I was married; four times happier than I was right after my husband left; and six times happier than I am when I'm getting a Botox injection, and I am barely 50 years old.

Life doesn't end at 50, and I feel as pretty today as I did walking down the runway at my Charm School graduation, and prettier than I ever did walking down the aisle and shaking like a leaf at one of my weddings. I will always prefer a little black dress to a long white gown, and I will continue to work out with Trainer Mike to make sure that I am still able to wear one at 72, like Holly Golightly most certainly is.

Johnny is married now, but we still meet for a drink at *The Grill* every so often so he can check on my progress and I can hear stories about his fairy tale marriage. I call him my "single-life guru," a moniker he brushes off with, "Aw shucks, ma'am, I'm just an old married guy who still likes to chat up a pretty girl." Nice to hear at 51.

I still consult with Poly-Ted on a regular basis too, and he has become one of my poly-paramours. I asked him once if he thought polyamory was a permanent state of being or just a journey back to a more enlightened version of serial-monogamy. He said it could be either or it could be both. I understand that as long as I am using Johnny's litmus test on fish the likelihood of me getting married again soon is slim, and I don't see the point in cutting bait on any fish I like until I meet someone worth abandoning the pond for. But I don't see myself going on for years with all these coded names plus numbers in my phone either, and I would like to lift the ban on Mikes soon because I saw a cute fish named Mike in my livewell the other day. Which makes me think about the original Mike, who I miss having as a friend to be the man when I need one, and who already seems on the verge of getting married again.

Which reminds me that I am still married, and see no reason to get divorced, since it's just a piece of paper which can't keep us apart as long as we own a business together and share parental responsibility for a nephew, any more than the piece of paper it would nullify could keep us together.

Which makes me think of Vicki who is living proof that you don't need a husband to have a life, and calls her David "a nice accessory that adds flash to an old, comfortable outfit."

Which reminds me of something Todd often says – that we could continue being in a part-time, non-committed relationship forever – and I sometimes think so too.

Which reminds me that my relationship with Todd lasts because he always goes away eventually, and I've never liked the way a fish smells when it's kept in the livewell too long.

Which brings to mind the final, tearful pages of *Breakfast at Tiffany's*, when Holly admits to being scared for the first time that she will go on forever not knowing what belongs to her until she has thrown it away.

Which makes me wonder, as I sometimes do, why I keep fishing when I am content with my large circle of friends and the fish I have in my livewell now, like Todd and Poly-Ted and the latest Mike.

And that leads me to think I should spend more time on dry land in the real world, and spend some of that time with Travis who is a man now, and a fish, which means he could jump out of my fishbowl at any time and swim out to sea, so it's up to me to help chart his course.

This doesn't feel like a fateful moment, so I'll saunter slowly past the fifty-yard line for now and know I've reached the goal when a feeling of ever-after washes over me like a karmic wave. Until then, halftime may be over but Football Bob was wrong. My life does not have a scoreboard or a time clock and important decisions DO NOT have to be made today.

Acknowledgments

All of the stories in FISHTAILS took place in the window of time between August of 2009 and June of 2011. Another year was spent editing, polishing and finding a publisher – all the while wondering if I should continue writing because more fish tales ensued. I chose to leave it as it is: a small slice of time in a significantly longer life.

I want to thank my editors Lee Sherry, Dawn Murphy, Alisa Cromer and Wendy Tokunaga, each of whom added something that made Fishtails a better book. My eagle-eye proofreaders Kathy McCarthy and Vicki Day were amazingly diligent at a thankless job. My primary fish muses Mike Bohrer, Todd Saba and Tom McReynolds gave me valuable insights into the mind of a fish, and were each in their own way remarkable supportive of the book's writing. I can't name all the wonderful writers I met at the Stanford Writer's Workshop or the San Francisco Writer's Conference, but the feedback and encouragement I received at both were indispensable.

The members of my book club – Suzanne Salata, Laura Schoennauer, Mary Lou Cardosa, Lee Sherry, Jan Schneider, Barbara Cohen, Chris Di Salvo, Georgie Huff and Vicki Day – put up with me changing the endings to the books we read year after year, and always said I should write my own book instead of rewriting the work of other authors. They were also the first beta readers of Fishtails (and it was a crude first draft) so I am forever grateful for their friendship and encouragement.

Photographer Kent Clemenco spent a day with me shooting fish in a salad bowl to get the cover shot just right. Only Kent can make minnows smile, and I am pleased to say that we released them into the Guadalupe River when the photo session was done. The people who made me look good were Mike Bohrer for his cover design, Charlotte Boccone for the logo typography, Nancy Cleary for the interior layout, and Julie Donnellan for the author photo. Authors Sandi Selvi and Julie Matsushima helped me navigate the sea of choices in the publishing industry that landed me at Wyatt-MacKenzie.

Finally, I want to thank all of the single women who called me with stories when they learned I had written this book. Fishtails could have been much longer, but I had to keep reminding myself that the book was complete and it was time to move on.

I am still single, now divorced, and all of the single men and women mentioned in the book remain unattached as well. Relationships don't start and end as cleanly as literature dictates they should, so many of the fish I released in Fishtails remain in my life today as friends, and the friends who found love in one of my stories lost it again before the book was through the first round of edits. Such is life.

The Author

Nanci Williams has been writing since the age of 6, when she acquired a typewriter and started publishing *The Cleveland Street News* with a circulation of 4 neighbors. By the age of 7, she discovered carbon paper and circulation expanded four-fold. As an adult, she made a career of writing ad copy, brochure copy, website content, and news releases for large corporations and small retailers, but *Fishtails* is her first full-length book. She splits her time between a fishbowl in downtown San Jose and a lake house in Paso Robles, and remains happily single. She is currently at work on a novel.

For more information, visit her Facebook page at www..facebook.com/fishtailsbook

CPSIA information can be obtained at www.ICGtesting.com
Printed in the USA
BVOW071841301012

304218BV00001B/1/P